BATTLE of BRITAIN

Last Look Back

BATTLE of BRITAIN

Last Look Back

Dilip Sarkar

Ramrod Publications

Contents

Dedication

For Anita

Other books by Dilip Sarkar:-

SPITFIRE SQUADRON: 19 Squadron at War, 1939-41
THE INVISIBLE THREAD: A Spitfire's Tale
THROUGH PERIL TO THE STARS
ANGRIFF WESTLAND
A FEW OF THE MANY: A Kaleidoscope of Memories
BADER'S TANGMERE SPITFIRES: The Untold Story, 1941
BADER'S DUXFORD FIGHTERS: The Big Wing Controversy
MISSING IN ACTION: Resting in Peace?
GUARDS VC: Blitzkrieg 1940
BATTLE OF BRITAIN: The Photographic Kaleidoscope, Volumes I,II, III & IV
FIGHTER PILOT: The Photographic Kaleidoscope
DOUGLAS BADER: An Inspiration in Photographs
JOHNNIE JOHNSON: Spitfire Top Gun, Part One

To receive early notification of the availability of our books, including highly collectable signed limited editions, please submit your details for inclusion on the Ramrod mailing list.

BATTLE OF BRITAIN: *Last Look Back*
© Dilip Sarkar, 2002
ISBN: 0-9538539-6-9

First published 2002 by Ramrod Publications, Bayhouse, 16 Kingfisher Close, St Peter's, Worcester WR4 3RY, ENGLAND. Tel & Fax: 01905 767735.
Email: anita@ramrodbooks.u-net.com.   www.battleofbritain.net/ramrodbooks

Layout and design by Ramrod Publications
Printed & bound in Great Britain by Aspect Design, 89 Newtown Road, Malvern, Worcs WR14 1PD

Acknowledgements

Clearly this book could not have been written without the enthusiastic co-operation of members of the Battle of Britain Fighter Association members featured in this book, and indeed the other veterans. We thank them all, one and all, for having the foresight to co-operate with me, especially in the early days when all I had was a ring binder, paper and pen, and absolutely no guarantee that there would ever be a tangible end result from my enthusiasm!

Certain friends continue to provide essential assistance, namely Mark Postlethwaite, Larry McHale, Alan Putland, Ray Loveslife-Brown, Robert Rudhall and Andrew Long.

My wife Anita is not only 'Ramrod Publications', the small operation that we founded together 10 years ago to make all of this possible, but also creates the domestic circumstances necessary for me to enjoy *two* demanding jobs! She should not underestimate what we have achieved, or indeed the contribution to history that has been made, in no small part due to her support.

Bibliography

There are certain books about the Battle of Britain which are not only essential references but have also inspired me significantly over the years. The following is not intended to be a comprehensive Battle of Britain bibliography, but a suggestion for further reading.

Battle of Britain Then & Now, Mk V, Edited by Winston Ramsey, After the Battle, 1989
The Blitz Then & Now, Vols I, II & III, Edited by Winston Ramsey, 1989 & 1990
Men of the Battle of Britain, Ken Wynn, Gliddon Books, 1989
Dowding & the Battle of Britain, Robert Wright, Corgi, 1970
Sir Keith Park, Dr Vincent Orange, Methuen, 1984
Aces High, Chris Shores & Clive Williams, 1994
RAF Squadrons, Wing Commander CG Jefford, Airlife, 1988
The Hardest Day, Dr Alfred Price, MacDonald & Jane's, 1979
Duel of Eagles, Group Captain Peter Townsend, Corgi, 1972
The Narrow Margin, Derek Wood & Derek Dempster, Arrow Books, 1969
Battle Over Britain, Francis K Mason, Aston Publications, 1990

Introduction

During the spring of 1940, German forces achieved an unprecedented lightning advance to the Channel coast, conquering on the way Belgium, Holland, Luxembourg and France. The tactics involved revolutionised warfare and comprised aircraft employed as flying artillery operating in support of fast moving armour and mechanised infantry. Already Poland, Norway and Denmark had fallen to the Nazis, and as the British Expeditionary Force, despite having won five Victoria Crosses, was evacuated back to 'Blighty' from the beaches around Dunkirk, it seemed that Hitler was invincible. Just pause for a moment to consider this fact: what was not achieved during five years of total war between 1914 – 1918, had this time around been delivered in just 60 days. The West was *stunned*, and it must be emphasised that France was considered amongst the most potent military powers of the time. Hitler's victory appeared absolute.

Having also suffered heavy losses during the Great War, during the 1930s America steadfastly pursued a foreign policy of 'Isolation from events in Europe'. Never again did American mothers want to send their sons to fight a far off war that they did not consider their concern. Furthermore, Stalin's communist Russia, although ideologically the natural enemy of Nazism, had signed a Non Aggression Pact with Germany, meaning that whilst Hitler plundered the West, he had no thrust from the East to fear. What Churchill later called Germany's 'soft under belly' was also secure given that fascist Italy was Hitler's friend. To the Southwest, Spain presented no threat as the fascist dictator General Franco, although sympathetic to Germany, was determined to remain neutral.

Across the English Channel, however, lay Britain, her army battered and bruised from the Fall of France, its tanks, artillery and other heavy equipment littering the route from Belgium's River Dyle to the French coast. It was considered most unlikely that the British Army could resist a German seaborne invasion. The Royal Navy was scattered around the world, protecting commonwealth territories, and it was unlikely that a striking force of warships could be concentrated quickly enough to act decisively against an invasion fleet. Nevertheless, Britain had made it clear that, although alone and in an apparently hopeless military situation, there was no question whatsoever of either surrendering to Nazi oppression or reaching any compromise.

The opportunity to invade Britain was an unexpected one for the German High Command. Suddenly, intoxicated by the scent of victory, serious consideration was given to this undertaking, as evidenced by Hitler's famous Directive Number 16:-

> I have decided to begin preparations for, and if necessary, to carry out the invasion of England.
>
> This operation is dictated by the necessity to eliminate Great Britain as a base from which war against Germany can be waged. If necessary the island can be occupied.

Aerial supremacy, however, was crucial to such an undertaking. The Commander-in-Chief of the *Luftwaffe, Reichsmarschall* Herman Göring boasted:-

> My *Luftwaffe* is invincible…. And so now we turn to England. How long will this one last – two, three weeks?

For the British, the prospect of Nazi soldiers goose-stepping down Pall Mall, as they had revelled in doing along the Champs Elyseé, their gaudy and tasteless swastika flags flying over Buckingham Palace, was unthinkable. Air Chief Marshal Sir Hugh Dowding was the Air Officer Commanding-in-Chief of RAF Fighter Command:-

> My strength has now been reduced to the equivalent of 36 squadrons…. we should be able to carry on the war single-handedly for some time, if not indefinitely.

All now looked to Fighter Command to retain control of British skies, and in so doing stave off the proposed German invasion. It was a challenge to which Fighter Command looked with optimism and, by close of play, would prove equal.

Churchill articulately placed Fighter Command's task into context when he made crystal clear exactly what was at stake, and what was now expected of the British people:-

The whole fury and might of the enemy must very soon be turned upon us. Hitler knows that he will have to break us in this island or lose the war. If we can stand up to him, all Europe may be free and the life of the world may move forward into broad sunlit uplands. But if we fail, then the whole world, including the United States, including all that we have known and cared for, will sink into the abyss of a new Dark Age made more sinister, and perhaps more protracted, by the lights of perverted science. Let us therefore brace ourselves to our duties, and so bear ourselves that, if the British Empire and Commonwealth last for a thousand years, men will still say 'This was their Finest Hour'.

Officially, the German effort to destroy Fighter Command began on July 10th, 1940, and opened with attacks on Channel shipping and coastal radar stations. Then Fighter Command's airfields were hammered, but just when the situation became critical for the beleaguered defenders, on September 7th, the Germans switched to attacking London. The intention was twofold. Firstly London was considered the only target capable of forcing Fighter Command to commit all of its fighters to battle, for destruction en masse by the waiting Me 109s, nearly all of which had been transferred to the Pas-de-Calais and command of *Luftflotte* 2 for this undertaking. Secondly it was believed that the heavy bombing of civilian areas would crush morale and extinguish the will to resist. The Germans were wrong on both counts. The change in targets at such a crucial moment provided Fighter Command the opportunity to repair its vital Sector Stations, and, far from throwing in the towel, Londoners won the admiration of the free world by declaring 'We can take it'. Indeed, the gutted ruins of formerly fine shops bore signs stating 'Business as usual', as the capital continued to function as the country's centre of communication and commerce. Far away across the Atlantic, many Americans, who had considered Britain's collapse inevitable, were being forced to think again.

Moreover, and contrary to the belief of German intelligence, Dowding's fighters were not, in fact, concentrated in the south to meet the main threat, but distributed throughout the country. True the reserve comprised squadrons that were training and making good losses suffered in the main combat area, but they were still effective units. Indeed, when the Germans attacked targets in Northeast England on August 15th, they were hacked apart by Spitfires and Hurricanes. This was a demoralising shock to the enemy aircrews who had been led to believe that there would be little opposition. Clearly, the boastful Göring had grossly underestimated the British.

The crescendo of battle came on September 15th, when London and other targets in the south of England were pounded day and night. German losses were heavy, however, and the RAF declared the day to be theirs. Although more recent research indicates that the number of German aircraft shot down was actually much lower than believed at the time, it was nevertheless a fact that many wrecked enemy machines littered the route to and from their targets. It was also fact that the enemy had yet to strike the decisive blow, and clearly could not sustain such high losses indefinitely.

After the events of September 30th, which saw further heavy losses inflicted on the enemy, the Germans had no choice but to discontinue using mass formations of bombers over England during daylight. Further attacks were to involve *Junkers 88s*, the only bomber considered able to hold its own against the RAF fighters, and only in *Gruppe* strength (up to 30 aircraft). Even then, the fast and heavily armed 88s still needed fighter protection to achieve success against targets connected with the British aircraft industry that represented the campaign's latest emphasis. Such targets, so late in the day, were not to have any effect on the RAF's ability to fight, however. It was now clear that the *Luftwaffe* could not achieve a strategic objective with tactical aircraft, the bomb capacity and range of which were insufficient for the task in hand. Conversely, the RAF fighters were being used in their intended role, that of short-range interceptors, which, it must be remembered, enjoyed the benefits of radar based early warning and the support network of Dowding's unique 'System'.

By now the summer had long since matured into autumn and weather conditions became increasingly unfavourable and unreliable for a seaborne invasion. Nevertheless, by night the German bombers wreaked havoc against British cities, nocturnal defences being in their infancy, but these targets were not going to decisively assist the requirement to destroy Fighter Command. By day, Me 109s swept over southern England, the fighter-bombers within their formations meaning that these incursions could not be ignored. Consequently Fighter Command was forced to mount standing patrols from dawn to dusk, and many survivors recall this final phase as the most exhausting. Although the fighters clashed frequently in what had become a war of attrition, Dowding's clever shepherding and preservation of his force, coupled with excellent aircraft supply and repair, and pilot replacement arrangements, meant that Fighter Command was always in a position to continue the fight.

Officially, the Battle of Britain finished on October 31st. It has been argued, however, that the German air offensive against Britain was not, in fact, over until May 1941, when the night *blitz* reached its zenith. These attacks, heavy though they were, were not going to force Britain to capitulate. Indeed, the increasing pathos towards the end of the *nachtangriff* was arguably intended to disguise the fact that Hitler's territorial ambitions had turned eastwards. The following month, the bulk of German forces would be transferred to the east and, in direct contravention of the supposed Nazi-Soviet Non Aggression Pact, unleashed against Russia.

Hitler's failure to defeat Fighter Command and invade England during 1940, did, as Churchill predicted, decide the war. When the Führer invaded Russia in June 1941, America was still a sleeping giant. The air war with England had become merely an irritating thorn, whilst on all other fronts Axis forces enjoyed the upper hand. If this situation had continued, it is possible that Germany could have defeated Russia, but the events of December 1941, changed everything. On December 7th, the Japanese surprised the American Fleet at Pearl Harbour and attacked with a force of 360 aircraft. The raid was a complete surprise, not least because a state of war did not exist between the two nations concerned. Following this crime, America declared war on Japan, and in turn, as an expression of support for its Far Eastern ally, Germany declared war on the United States. Hitler was now also at war with the two most immense and potentially powerful nations in the world. Little England, still defiant and free, became virtually a stepping stone on which American and Commonwealth military resources could be stockpiled and from which the liberation of Europe could be launched.

It cannot be emphasised enough that Britain was the only country that had held out against the *Blitzkrieg* in 1940, and the only nation that could now play host to an Allied invasion force. When that liberating Allied army eventually crossed the Channel, on June 6th, 1944, and penetrated deeper into Nazi occupied territory, it would discover terror, murder and mayhem on an evil scale hitherto unknown by the civilised world. If not for the determination and commitment to democracy steadfastly reflected by the British people in those dark and apparently hopeless days of 1940, the fate of this island under Nazi rule would have been no different to that of the oppressed peoples of mainland Europe. That this terrible fate was averted is due completely to the men and women of RAF Fighter Command. Had they lost, there is no doubt that ultimately Hitler would have harnessed nuclear energy for military purposes and perfected the inter-continental ballistic missile on which his scientist were working at the war's end. Indeed, on March 25th, 1945, U-234 sailed from Bergen bound for Japan. Aboard were two Japanese officers and several civilian engineering specialists together with a cargo of uranium oxide (necessary in the production of atomic weapons) and an Me 262 jet fighter in component parts. On May 6th, however, in anticipation of a German collapse, Japan declared itself free of all treaties made with Hitler, who by then had committed suicide in Berlin, and made clear its intention to fight on alone. Two days later Germany surrendered, unconditionally, as a result of which, and taking Japan's former statement into account, the commander of U-234 immediately placed both his Japanese passengers under arrest and surrendered his submarine in accordance with instructions issued by the victorious Allies. Had Japan received the uranium oxide, it would have been too late for any action given that the Second World War was ended in August 1945, when the Americans dropped two atomic bombs on Japan. The prospect, however, of the Nazis being in possession of uranium oxide, and not only possessing nuclear knowledge but making real steps to pass that advantage to Japan, is a chilling thought.

The point is that had Britain fallen in 1940, there is no doubt that ultimately the advances in nuclear science would have lengthened Hitler's arm to reach even the United States. No Isolationism would have saved America then. So, when we examine the wider implications of a Nazi victory in 1940, Fighter Command's victory becomes even more remarkable. The realisation dawns regarding just how much we all still owe those who fought for freedom. Back then, Churchill himself paid homage to Fighter Command, which had lost over 500 aircrew during the epic 16 week conflict:-

The gratitude of every home in our island, in our Empire, and indeed throughout the world, except in the abodes of the guilty, goes out to the British airmen, who, undaunted by odds, unwearied in their constant challenge and mortal danger, are turning the tide of world war by their prowess and devotion. Never in the field of human conflict was so much owed by so many to so few.

Typifying the spirit of those who fought, however, Squadron Leader Brian Lane DFC, the 23-year old Commanding Officer of 19 Squadron, remarked:-

When we heard the Prime Minister's speech, we thought he was talking about our Mess bills!

Sadly Lane was killed in action on December 13th, 1942, and remains Missing in Action to this day. His apparent modesty, however, is typical of the attitude reflected by survivors of 'Churchill's Few' today, over 60 years after their dogfights took place high over England. All are now pensioners in advanced age, in their 80s and even 90s. In the main, all are matter-of-factly modest about their august experiences, and in particular their own contribution. When enticed, they will talk freely of general recollections, but their inner feelings often remained closely guarded secrets. All, without a doubt, are, however, intensely proud to have fought for their country in that darkest and yet finest hour. All are proud to wear the tie of the Battle of Britain Fighter Association, featuring the shape of Great Britain and the rosette to the 1939-45 Star awarded to the Few, membership of which is exclusively restricted to Battle of Britain aircrew. Those who served in support rolls too share this great pride and bond, and there is again no doubt that their less glamorous contribution was essential. Indeed, as Lord Dowding himself once said, 'Think of us not as individuals but as a Battle of Britain team'. Fortunately for us it was that 'home team' that took away the ultimate cup, for these were *real* heroes, men and women who bravely faced shot, shell and bomb with a steely resolve. Men like Flight Lieutenant James Brindley Nicholson of 249 Squadron, who climbed back into the cockpit of his blazing Hurricane to shoot down a German aircraft. For this 'signal act of valour' he became the only fighter pilot to be awarded the Victoria Cross in World War Two. Women like WAAF Sergeant Joan Mortimer who marked every unexploded bomb at Biggin Hill Sector Station with a red flag, and whose courage was recognised by the Military Medal. Real heroes, to whom we owe so much, but know so little.

Years ago I set out to record the memories of the Few. My resources were minimal, to say the least, sponsorship nil. What I lacked in those departments, however, I made up for in enthusiasm and commitment, which was no bad thing given that this self-imposed quest had to be fitted in around my demanding full time job as a serving police officer and our young family. The result has not only been 17 published works but, more importantly, privileged friendships forged amongst the Few and their families, memories of happy meetings and time spent in their company. The aim of this book is to present some of these recollections, which are in the main those of the 'also rans', as Battle of Britain pilot Peter Fox describes himself, those who have not sought publicity or recognition, those whose stories are not common knowledge. To all of them I give thanks, not only for their co-operation and friendship, but also for what they did when half my age, and a quarter of their own ages now.

Dilip Sarkar, Worcester, June 2002

Note: Ranks used are as during the Battle of Britain. Unless otherwise indicated, photographs have been either passed into my collection by the veterans concerned, or have actually been taken by myself.

Chapter One

Sergeant David Cox

The pilots of Fighter Command in 1940 had followed various routes to the cockpit. Some were regular RAF officers and NCOs, whilst others were either auxiliaries or reservists. The auxiliaries tended to be young men of independent means, who flew for pleasure at weekends and served in locally raised units. Reservists tended towards those of a grammar school education, and these-air minded young men were taught to fly in their spare time. Others came from University Air Squadrons. All would make essential replacement pilots when war came.

Reservists were mobilised in August and September 1939, completing their Service Flying and prior to joining fighter squadrons. Before the war, pilots fresh from training school were given operational training by their squadron. When squadrons became engaged, however, and replacements were needed quickly, this was no longer possible.

Although Air Chief Marshal Dowding had been against the formation of dedicated Operational Training Units on the grounds that he could not afford the luxury, he soon had no choice but to expand existing arrangements. Courses were consequently reduced in length and content as these hard-pressed units worked to achieve the necessary monthly quota of newly trained pilots. After May 1940, instruction was often provided by pilots who had survived the fighting in France, and who passed on their knowledge of operational conditions and tactics.

The professional RAF men of the regular service, however, at first looked down at both the auxiliaries, for who flying was an exciting hobby, and the part-time reservists. Promotion in the comparatively small pre-war service was slow, it often taking professional Sergeants many years to reach that exulted rank. All aircrew volunteers automatically became Sergeants, however, so at first there was no mean amount of animosity between the older professional airmen whose Mess was suddenly shared by youngsters, many of them still teenagers, of equal rank.

David George Samuel Cox, from Cambridge, had attended Bournemouth School and joined the RAFVR whilst working as a solicitor's clerk. Called up on September 1st, 1939, he completed his flying training and was posted to 19 Squadron, at Duxford, on May 23rd, 1940. The 20-year old was this proud regular unit's first VR pilot, and it was the Squadron's task to make him combat ready:-

> When I joined 19 Squadron, I was engaged on Operation DYNAMO, the air operation in support of the Dunkirk evacuation and was operating out of Hornchurch. Because I had not received any Spitfire training, however, I was unable to participate, so was given the job of ferrying replacement Spitfires to Hornchurch or testing those that had been repaired.

> On May 28th, I was testing a Spitfire for radio trouble but when I prepared to land I found that the undercarriage would not fully retract, it stuck half way. After trying unsuccessfully for some time to rectify the situation, which included turning the aircraft on its back to try and take the weight off the 'pins', I had no alternative but to land with the undercart so stuck. Later, the Engineering Officer jacked the Spitfire up in a hangar and found the undercarriage to work perfectly. The

result was that the Commanding Officer, Squadron Leader Phillip Pinkham AFC, endorsed my logbook as follows:-

On August 10ᵗʰ 1940, Sergeant Cox was charged at Duxford with damaging one of His Majesty's aircraft, namely a Spitfire, through landing with the undercarriage incompletely lowered. The Station CO Duxford (Wing Commander AB Woodhall) directed that he be admonished and ordered me to make this entry.

I deeply resented this and at the time it soured my attitude towards the RAF. During February 1941, when things were quiet, I went to see Squadron Leader Brian Lane DFC, who had replaced Pinkham as CO in September 1940, when the latter was killed in action, and told him just how unjust I felt the endorsement to be as I had done my best to get the undercarriage down. He said that he would look into the matter. Later I heard from the Squadron Adjutant that Squadron Leader Lane had taken up the matter at Group HQ and had even made a formal personal visit. The result came through several months later when 'Cancelled' was written in red ink across the endorsement. Squadron Leader Lane added below it:-

Entry made in error. No disciplinary action was taken, as accident not attributable to pilot.

It appears that Squadron Leader Lane discovered that there had been similar accidents, all caused by an air lock which had been removed by the shock of landing, hence why the undercarriage worked perfectly in the hangar. This represents a perfect example of what a fine squadron commander and man Brian Lane was, that he should go to so much trouble on my behalf, a junior 'VR' pilot. He was always kind and considerate to all, however lowly their rank, and he was undoubtedly one of the finest squadron commanders I served under.

No 19 Squadron, the first unit to receive the Spitfire back in August 1938, was based at Fowlmere Farm, the satellite of Duxford Sector Station, near Cambridge, in 12 Group. Early on in the Battle of Britain, Duxford's squadrons often flew daily to aerodromes on the East Coast, such as Coltishall, from where they provided standing patrols over Channel bound convoys. The fighting, however, was taking place further south, particularly over the Dover area, which became appropriately known as 'Hellfire Corner'. Anxious for 12 Group to get some action, on

August 13th, the Group Commander, Air Vice-Marshal Leigh-Mallory, arranged for 'B' Flight of 19 Squadron to fly across to Eastchurch, near Sheerness, from where the Spitfires were to participate in an attack on German E-boats near Calais. In an example of the Luftwaffe's poor intelligence, Eastchurch (which was not an important sector or indeed even a fighter station) was heavily bombed. David remembers:-

> I was awakened by the bombing at about 0730. I rushed out of my room, which was in a wooden hut, into a corridor where I met Flight Sergeant Tofts, a pre-war professional airman who was in charge of the servicing of 'B' Flight's aircraft. He grabbed me by the arm and we ran into the only brick shelter available, a urinal, and Tofts pushed me to the floor, saying "This is no time to be squeamish, lad!" Apparently 250 bombs were dropped and the airfield was strafed. There were 30 odd casualties although fortunately none from 19 Squadron.

Fowlmere Farm, from where David Cox flew with 19 Squadron during the Battle of Britain and as it appeared through the lens of Andrew Long's camera in more recent times.

The proposed attack against the E-boats was cancelled, and 'B' Flight returned to Fowlmere. On August 15th, Sergeant Cox was amongst the 19 Squadron pilots scrambled:-

The Squadron was scrambled to intercept a raid on Martlesham Heath airfield. The attack was carried out by some 25 Me 110s of *Erprobungsgruppe* 210, led by their brilliant commander *Hauptmann* Rubensdörffer. The enemy were completely undetected until only a few minutes from the target. Only three Hurricanes of 17 Squadron managed to get airborne before the 110s arrived over the airfield. Our chances of intercepting the raid were nil, taking into consideration that Fowlmere to Martlesham was 60 air miles. Taking an optimistic speed for our Spitfires as 300 mph, it would take 12 minutes from take off to reach Martlesham. I doubt that at 2,000 feet our troublesome cannon-armed Mk IBs were capable of that speed anyway, as maximum speed was not reached until 19,000 feet. I would suggest that 280 mph was the maximum speed achievable at the given height, but even at 300 mph 19 Squadron could not achieve the impossible.

It was the start of increasing problems between 11 and 12 Groups. The System provided for 11 Group to make the forward interception, and whilst the fighters were up it was the responsibility of 12 Group to cover the 11 Group airfields. 12 Group, however, felt that 11 Group was attempting to hog the battle by only calling for assistance when absolutely necessary, by which time, as on August 15th, when it was too late given time, speed and distance. On August 26th, 19 Squadron was called upon to patrol the 11 Group Sector Station at Debden, as David remembers:-

We were instructed by 11 Group to patrol at 10,000 feet, but the actual raid came in at 1,000 feet. As 19 Squadron was nine thousand feet higher and above a complete 10/10ths covering of cloud, we saw nothing of what went on. Apparently the Observer Corps had reported a raid incoming at 1,000 feet, but the 11 Group controllers assumed this to be a mistake and vectored us to Angels 10 (height measured in thousands of feet). The subsequent intelligence report stated that 'the Spitfires from Fowlmere were slow in getting off the ground', which was absolutely not the case.

On August 31st, Fighter Command suffered its highest losses during the Battle of Britain:-

We of 19 Squadron were caught on the hop! Most of us were still in bed as the Squadron was in a state of 'Stood Down'. We got a panic message to scramble at once. I put on my flying boots and jacket over my pyjamas. We took off at about 0800 and climbed south to Angels 17. It was jolly cold up there as the flying jacket only came down to my waist!

We soon sighted the enemy, about 30 *Dorniers* escorted by a large number of Me 110s above and behind. I was No 3 in Blue Section, which was led by Flying Officer James Coward. We were above and behind the bombers but below the 110s. We were put into echelon starboard and dived onto a section of bombers. Before I could open fire I was attacked by the 110s, so I took evasive action, a very, very sharp left-hand climbing turn, after which I found myself alone and no longer in contact with the Squadron.

I then climbed up to about 20,000 feet and flew southeast. Over Clacton I saw about 20 – 30 110s milling around in a left-hand circle, about 2,000 feet below me. I dived onto the circle and fired at one 110 that had got detached from the formation. My cannons operated perfectly as I was keeping a straight line without turning. The 110 turned sharply to port and then dived away steeply with his port engine belching black smoke. I was then attacked by four other 110s and so, being out of ammunition, got the hell out of it!

Apparently the 110 that I shot down belonged to II/ZG 76, the crew of which were both rescued from the sea and captured.

When I got back to Fowlmere I landed over the smoking remains of 19-year old Pilot Officer Aeberhardt's Spitfire. Having had some success in this engagement he crashed on landing due to being unaware of certain damage to his machine, flaps I think. After the war I visited his grave several times at Whittlesford churchyard. At first it was on its own with a large headstone and was well looked after. After about 20 years it became overgrown and obviously uncared for. I tidied it up myself and put some flowers on it. The last time I visited, Pilot Officer Aeberhardt's remains had been moved to lie amongst the other RAF graves and was, like them, carefully tended.

From September 7th onwards, 19 Squadron flew as part of the so-called Duxford Wing, a 'balbo' of five fighter squadrons with the remarkable legless Squadron Leader Douglas Bader (CO of 242 Squadron) at its head. The Wing was created in response to Bader's appreciation of a combat fought by 242 on August 30th. The Hurricanes had been scrambled from Duxford to patrol North Weald Sector Station whilst the 11 Group squadrons therefrom were in action further south. On patrol over Essex at 15,000 feet, 242 Squadron was then vectored 340°. This change of course was in response to some 60 He 111s, escorted by Me 110s, heading for the aircraft factories at Radlett and Hatfield, north of the Thames. Squadron Leader Bader found that he enjoyed a height advantage over the lower group of enemy aircraft, which were also down sun of his Hurricanes. Being perfectly positioned, 242 Squadron struck and later claimed the destruction of numerous enemy aircraft.

In what was 242 Squadron's first mass combat of the Battle of Britain, Bader and his pilots were apparently oblivious to the presence of Spitfires and Hurricanes from other RAF squadrons. These included the experienced Nos 1 (Hurricanes) and 222 (Spitfires) Squadrons, as evidenced by combat reports preserved at the Public Records Office (Air 50). The damage inflicted upon the enemy was not, therefore, the solo execution that 242 believed, although the Squadron's combat claims were accepted without exception. On the basis of this experience, Squadron Leader Bader argued the case that if he had been in command of more fighters than just the 12 of his own Squadron, more damage could have been inflicted. Bader's theory was gained the support of Air Vice-Marshal Leigh-Mallory who arranged that Bader would lead a 12 Group 'Wing', initially comprising the Hurricanes of 242 and 310 (Czech) Squadrons, and the Spitfires of 19. On September 7th, Bader sallied forth with 35 fighters behind him, but caught on the climb and therefore at a tactical disadvantage the engagement was not a success. Nevertheless the experiment was continued.

On September 15th, the 'Big Wing', now also including the Hurricanes of 302 (Polish) and the Spitfires of 611 Squadrons, arrived over the capital *en masse*. Sergeant Cox was amongst the 60 12 Group fighters:-

> Now that was pretty inspiring, you must admit, all of us following Bader and arriving over the capital like that! I well remember the words of Bobby Oxspring, then a Flying Officer in an 11 Group Spitfire squadron, 66, exclaiming what a wonderful sight it was to see us appear. We must have given the German aircrews, who had been told that we were down to our last handful of fighters, one hell of a shock!

On September 27th, there were three major attacks mounted against

London, and another raid headed for Filton in the West Country. David Cox:-

I had jumped into the nearest Spitfire, X4237, 'QV – L', as mine would not start. This aircraft was nearly always flown by Sergeant Plzak, the six feet and six inches tall Czech who had dubbed me 'Little Boy'. To save time I buckled on his parachute which was already in the cockpit – more of that later!

19 Squadron took off just before noon and we were the Duxford Wing's top cover. It was in the area of Dover that a large number of Me 109s attacked us from above. After some hectic moments avoiding being shot down, I found myself more or less on my own between Ashford and Folkestone. Towards the latter I saw a Hurricane being set upon by four 109s, but before I could provide assistance, which was my intention having got within a few hundred yards of the scrap, the Hurricane went down in a vertical dive. This was a 242 Squadron aircraft flown by Pilot Officer Michael Homer DFC, who was killed when his machine crashed at Sittingbourne.

The four 109s then turned their attention to me. They knew their stuff as two got above me and two below. Naturally I had some hectic moments of turning this way and that as they came at me in attacks from all directions. I remember doing a lot of firing, but it was more in the hope of frightening them or raising my morale than in any real hope of shooting anything down!

All of a sudden there was a loud bang in the cockpit and for a second or two I was dazed. When I resumed normal there was a lot of smoke and my Spitfire was in a steep dive. I grabbed the control column and went up in a steep climb. As I lost flying speed I opened the hood, turned the aircraft over, undid my straps and fell out, quickly pulling the rip chord of my parachute. When the canopy opened it gave me a severe jolt, and several days later a lot of bruises showed on my chest and shoulders. Remember that the parachute harness was set for a man of six-and-a-half feet tall, I was lucky not to fall out of it!

As I floated down a 109 came and had a look at me and then flew off. It was then that I felt a lot of pain in my right leg and saw lots of holes in my flying boots out of which blood was oozing. Ground observers say that I took about 15 minutes to come down as I was so high up – I know that it was jolly cold up there when I came out of the aeroplane.

I landed in the corner of a ploughed field near a farm at Walsford, near Ashford. Two farm hands carried me into the farmhouse. By this time I was feeling rather rough and must have looked it as the farmer handed me a bottle of whisky, from which I took a large swig. I was later taken to hospital at Walsford where a surgeon from Folkestone Hospital extracted several large pieces of cannon shell from just below my kneecap down into my ankle. I was in hospital about six weeks and off flying until December 1940. By coincidence, the next time I was shot down was on Friday 27th June, 1941, again in a Spitfire coded 'QV–L'!

Pilot Officer Eric Burgoyne, who was killed in this action, is buried in the churchyard at Burghfield. I have visited his grave, which is in a quiet spot underneath a large oak tree. He joined 19 Squadron on the same day as Pilot Officer Sutherland, Sergeant Roden and myself. Of the four I am the only survivor.

Waiting. 12 Group pilots of 242 Squadron await the call to scramble with their CO, Squadron Leader Douglas Bader (seated, second right), Duxford, 1940.

So ended David Cox's Battle of Britain, during which he destroyed an Me 110 and an Me 109. So, all these years later, what does he think of the controversial 'Big Wing', which, we now know, literally flew in the face of the Commander-in-Chief's System:-

> When the Wing went into action the Spitfires kept the escorting fighters busy whilst the Hurricanes went for the bombers. This was right, I think, as the Spitfires were better suited from a performance perspective to tackle the 109s, whereas the Hurricanes would have been disadvantaged. Five squadrons were too many, I think. Three was OK, but why not three Spitfire squadrons, all therefore with identical performance? Spitfire squadrons would have made the allotted patrol lines faster and with the advantage of more height. That having been said, I do think that 11 Group could often have called for us earlier on. There is no doubt that many 11 Group personnel blamed the Wing's late arrival for their airfields being bombed. This caused bad feeling even between pilots. Even as late as the 1960s I got punched on the nose at a pub in Grimsby by a former 41 Squadron pilot when he discovered that I had flown with the Big Wing!

On April 21st, 1945, David Cox was sent to Burma and given command of a Spitfire Wing. In five years this NCO VR pilot had risen to Wing Commander, had become a fighter 'ace' (having also served with distinction in North Africa) and received a DFC and Bar. Having also been decorated by the French with a *Croix de Guerre*, Wing Commander Cox left the RAF in 1946, and went home to his wife, Pat. Like the other veterans featured in this book, David never forgot his combat flying, which must surely represent the most exciting, but uncertain, period of their lives. On September 15th, 1980, the MOD permitted David Cox to fly over London as second pilot in a front line RAF Lightning jet interceptor. Forty years previously David had been over London in a Spitfire, in very different circumstances! In 1988, he participated in a 'Jim'll Fix It' television programme, during which David flew in the Grace Spitfire, ML407. It came as no surprise to hear that David had taken the controls, but how could we, we mortals who have never flown to battle in a Spitfire, imagine the myriad of nostalgic emotions that this remarkable man felt at that awesome moment?

David Cox was amongst my earliest correspondents, and this chapter was written from the bulging file of letters arising and from notes made during our various meetings at his comfortable Berkshire home. Today,

David is 82, and cares for his beloved Pat, the couple having been married for 62 years. Long may that partnership continue!

Wing Commander DGSR Cox DFC & Bar pictured at home by the author in 1995.

Chapter Two

Sergeant Geoffrey Stevens

Geoffrey Stevens was also a VR pilot called to full-time service on September 1st, 1939. The 22-year old completed his flying training and learned to fly Hurricanes at No 6 Operational Training Unit in July 1940. The following month saw him posted to 151 Squadron at North Weald, but having been engaged throughout the Battle of France and the struggle for Britain to date, the unit was rested soon after. Sergeant Stevens courageously volunteered to remain in the combat area, and so was posted to 213 Squadron at Tangmere.

At 1610 hours on September 30th, 1940, Squadron Leader Duncan MacDonald's 213 Squadron was scrambled from Tangmere, the famous Sector Station on the South coast. The Hurricanes were initially vectored to intercept a raid of 200 plus bandits that had crossed the coast two minutes previously. Sergeant Geoffrey Stevens recalls an unexpected turn of events:-

> Quite abruptly and without warning we were ordered to turn 180° and told "Buster" (travel at full throttle, make all haste). R/T talk between our 'Bearskin Leader' and Control elicited the information that it was a 60 plus raid (returning from an attack on Yeovil). We soon saw the enemy, first as dots that gradually developed into a mixture of He 111s

and Me 110s, and some Me 109s that were, as usual, above us. We were at about the same height as the bombers and 110s. I initially went for one of the latter, but he evaded by executing a spiral dive. I did not follow as I wished to retain height, but then saw a formation of three He 111s below me, so I dived on them, selecting the left-hand aircraft as my target. I got a fair amount of stick from all three gunners and opened with quite a long burst. However, I was travelling too fast and broke away left and downwards. I pulled back into a steep, almost vertical climb at full throttle, intending to come around again for another go, feeling quite sure that I had silenced the gunner in the aircraft I had fired at. At this point, near the top of the climb, the belly of an Me 110 slid into view, going from right to left. I opened up and continued climbing. I saw strikes all along the underside, but I had reached the point of stall and at that moment ran out of ammunition. I fell out of the skies, as the saying goes, and as there was no point in returning to the fray I let the aircraft dive. This was very nearly my undoing as I had built up too much speed and had great difficulty in getting out of the dive. The airscrew over-revved and sprayed oil all over the windscreen but thankfully I made it by about 100 feet. Later, the airframe fitter told me that several wooden slats which ran underside and aft of the cockpit had been stoved in by my pull out.

In this particular engagement, 213 had met the enemy at about 1700 hours over Portland. For no loss, Squadron Leader Macdonald and Flying Officer Kellow each destroyed an Me 110, whilst Sub-Lieutenant Jeram, a Fleet Air Arm pilot seconded to Fighter Command, probably destroyed another. Sergeants Stevens and Barrow both claimed 110s as damaged, and Pilot Officer Atkinson destroyed an Me 109. As 213 broke away, Squadron Leader John Sample's 504 Squadron hit the raiders, south of Portland, and so the battle continued to rage (and of which more can be read both elsewhere in this book and specifically in my *Angriff Westland*).

On October 17th, Geoffrey was in trouble again, as he recalled for me many years later:-

We of 213 Squadron were scrambled late in the afternoon, getting on for 1700 hours, and as we climbed away from Tangmere I remember thinking that I wished Flight Lieutenant Jackie Sing (commander of 'A' Flight) was leading us, as in my opinion he was the best. Neither did we have a tail end Charlie, for reasons that escaped me.

We climbed to about 17,000 feet when I noticed anti-aircraft shells bursting ahead and below. I reported this and at about the same time we had a course correction starboard. As we turned I saw strikes on Red Two, just ahead of me. We were flying the stupid close formation 'vic' of three aircraft in line astern (I was Yellow 2). Simultaneously I was hit in the engine by three or four cannon shells. The rev counter went off the clock and smoke and flames enveloped the outside. The standard practice if hit was to get out of the action as quickly as one could. I therefore shoved the stick over and went into a spiral dive. Flames, smoke and glycol fumes were everywhere, and I went down switching off everything I could think of.

I entered cloud at about 10,000 feet, coming out at 5,000 feet whilst preparing to bale out. The flames appeared to have stopped. I lifted up my goggles to have a look round and saw that I was over a town. I knew that if I baled out my aircraft would cause some severe damage, possibly loss of life. A field containing an AA gun was within gliding distance and so I opted for a forced-landing.

I did not appear to be in any immediate danger at this stage and so settled into a straight glide towards the field. Having sorted everything out in my mind, knowing exactly what I was going to do, I was dismayed to see what I have since described as electric light bulbs, but what were in fact tracer shells, going past my cockpit. Looking in my rear view mirror I saw a yellow nosed Me 109 on my tail. Without power, evasive action is limited, especially with so little height to play with. I used rudder to skid out of the German's sights, and am told that fortunately he'd been chased off by another Hurricane. I had lost height, however.

The effect of this on my carefully planned approach was disastrous. I opened the hood and blinded myself with glycol fumes. I put my goggles on again, but by this time I was very low, about 100 feet, travelling much too fast and in the wrong position for an approach to the field. Everything was wrong! I did a steep left-handed turn towards the field and slammed the Hurricane onto the ground, it was all I could do. It was unfortunate that I had been forced to choose the one approach that ended up with my wing root against a four feet thick tree stump. The aircraft shot into the air and over onto its back, into a sort of marsh. With all that had gone on leading up to this, I had omitted to lock the sliding cockpit hood open, and my harness back. The hood consequently slammed shut and I was propelled forward upon impact with some

Sergeant Stevens (right) and an unknown pilot during operational training.

force, cutting my head on the reflector gunsight.

I was now hanging upside down with blood running down my face. I could smell the petrol leaking out everywhere and hear the hissing of the cooling engine in the wet marsh. Otherwise everything seemed dead quiet. I tried to open the hood but it was useless. I was expecting the aircraft to go up in flames at any time and seemed powerless to effect an escape. I carefully released my straps and let myself down so that I lay on my back on top of the cockpit hood. I think that this was more to do *something* than continue hanging upside down doing nowt!

Although it seemed like an age, assistance actually came very quickly. People seemed to come from no where, including the Army. One helpful farmer got himself a corner post with a pointed metal end and rammed it through the Perspex hood. Had I still been hanging upside down it would have gone straight through my head, as it was it went just past my nose! To cut a long story short, one wing was lifted enough to allow the hood to slide back. The small clearance from the ground was sufficient for me, I was out of the wrecked Hurricane like a bullet from a gun! I'd never moved so fast in my life!

When I got out I could not stand up because the stick had come back and whacked my knee and I was somewhat shaken. However, with two men supporting me on each arm we made it to HQ and I remember

being amazed at the number of people there. As we walked up the field it was a crescent of people all looking to the centre. I only mention this because shaken though I was it left a clear impression that I can remember to this day.

They took me to Ashford Hospital, and later the soldiers returned and invited me to join them for a drink that night. Although I was willing the doctor was having none of it!

It is believed that 213 Squadron had clashed with the Me 109s of JG 77, flying out of Marquise, which were engaged on a *Freie Hunt*. In a classic example of overclaiming caused by the confusion created by a large number of fleeting fighters, seven 109 pilots claimed to have destroyed Hurricanes. In fact, only three were lost. It is possible that Geoffrey Stevens was shot down by *Gefrieter* Karl Raisinger of 3/JG 77. Just eight days later, Raisinger's 109 was hit in both the engine and radiator by an RAF fighter, forcing him to crash land near Saltdean.

Although safe, the young German was captured and spent the rest of a long war in captivity.

It must have been 1993 when first I contacted Geoffrey Stevens, during my research for *Angriff Westland*. My friend Ken Wakefield had already written about the raids against the West Country on September 25th & 27th 1940, and I intended to write about the two subsequent attacks on September 30th & October 7th. Geoffrey's combat experience on September 30th was included in a rich tapestry of first-hand accounts, and it was also the start of our friendship. Over the years since I have been privileged to have Geoffrey and his family present at many of our book launches and other events. His fighting spirit is evident given that on one occasion Geoffrey has joined us even though his only means of mobility was a motorised 'buggy'. On other occasions he has entered Worcester Guildhall using two sticks. In fact, on at least two occasions he had reluctantly declined invitations on the grounds of ill health, only to arrive unexpected on the day, such was his resolve to be present and provide support. Looking at the man today whilst bearing the experiences recounted here only increases respect and admiration.

Geoffrey Stevens at a recent Ramrod book launch (Andrew Long)

Chapter Three

Sergeants Denis Nichols & Peter Fox

Writing about yet more VR Sergeants, Denis 'Nick' Nichols and Peter Fox, emphasises just how many such pilots fought in the Battle of Britain. Without them it would have been impossible to make good losses, so clearly the far-sightedness that led to the creation of this part-time force paid off.

'Nick' had joined the VR in 1938, and completed his elementary flying training at Sywell in Northamptonshire. On September 1st, 1939, he too was called to full time service along with many other reservists, including Peter Fox and Ken Wilkinson. The threesome would go through their service flying training together. Having completed this at Montrose, on September 1st, 1940, Nichols and Fox moved on to No 6 OTU at Sutton Bridge, where they learned to fly the Hurricane, whilst Wilkinson (more of whom later) went to 7 OTU and Spitfires at Hawarden. Just a fortnight later, on September 15th, Sergeants Nichols and Fox, both of whom were 19, reported to 56 Squadron at RAF Boscombe Down in Dorset. The day afterwards, these two young fighter pilots were introduced to the grim realities of service on an operational fighter squadron when they performed duty as pall bearers at the funeral of a fellow NCO pilot who had been accidentally killed during dogfight practice.

Sergeant Peter Fox

56 Squadron was a regular fighter squadron with a proud tradition dating back to the Great War. Like 151, the other North Weald Hurricane squadron of the time, 56 had not only fought in France but was also heavily engaged throughout the early part of the Battle of Britain. Casualties had been high, however, and some fine airmen lost, men like Flight Lieutenant Percy 'Mouse' Weaver DFC, who failed to return from an engagement on August 31st. The following day, 56 was rested and sent to recuperate at Boscombe Down in 10 Group. Replacement pilots were received there and these 'sprogs' had the opportunity to receive further training by the Squadron. As Sergeants Nichols and Fox would soon discover, the prospect of combat over the West Country remained a distinct possibility.

On September 30th, the Germans made their last massed formation raid in daylight. The target was the Westland Aircraft Factory at Yeovil in Somerset. Unfortunately, however, cloud obscured the target, leading to an unfortunate navigational error that led to bombs cascading not on the intended target but on the nearby town of Sherborne in Dorset. Amongst the RAF fighters scrambled in response was 56 Squadron, and Sergeant Fox would soon catch his first glimpse of the enemy:-

I just couldn't believe it. There were about 40 He 111s of KG55, together with escorting Me 110s, approaching Lyme Bay, inbound. I selected one of the rearmost bombers, aimed firstly at one engine, pressed the gun button and sprayed across to the other. The enemy aircraft slowed significantly and peeled off to port. I followed, still firing, when suddenly there was an explosion and I noted that there was little left of my instrument panel! Fortunately my hood was already half open, which prevented any chance of it jamming shut in the event of the cockpit being so damaged. I broke to starboard, upwards and away, with all controls apparently functioning correctly. I got over land at 3,000 feet and was wondering whether I could make the coastal airfield at Warmwell (near Weymouth), when I saw flames coming up between my legs. I don't think that I even thought about my next action, which was to instinctively roll the kite upside down and release my harness. I then saw my feet still above me, and the Hurricane above my feet, presumably stalled. Where was the rip chord? I told myself to calm down, and pulled the 'D' ring straightaway. I had never before pulled a rip chord, never seen one pulled, never seen a parachute packed, and never had any instruction! The 'D' ring was flung into the air, followed by some wire. Obviously I had broken it! I then felt the tug of the pilot chute followed almost immediately by the wrench of the main parachute. I was safe! The next second I was aware of an 'enemy', which I assumed was going to shoot me. It was, however, my flaming Hurricane, which literally missed me by inches! The kite slowly screwed round, going into a steeper and steeper dive until almost vertical, aimed directly at the cross-hedges of four fields to the Northeast of a wood towards which I was drifting. The aircraft hit the cross-hedges spot on, a short pause then a huge explosion followed by another pause before flames shot up to a great height. I'm glad that I wasn't in it!

I was safe again but didn't feel it as the sea looked rather close and I didn't want to end up swimming. I then recalled a film about a German parachutist, which had shown how if you pulled the parachute lines on one side or the other, the direction was slipped off accordingly. I tried, but which side I don't know as I could not see which way I was drifting. I certainly could not think aerodynamically at that moment! Leave well alone, I thought! I was safe again, then, blood! Trickling down my right leg. I tried to lift my right leg to see, but couldn't. I'd met aircrew who had lost limbs but could still feel extremities that were no longer there. My leg must have been shot off and would crumble beneath me upon landing! I was getting close to the ground and worried about my 'shot off' leg when I remembered the story of a pilot being shot in the foot by the Home Guard. "BRITISH!" I shouted at the top of my voice. I pulled hard as my parachute clipped a tree on the edge of a wood. Upon landing I just fell over gently, when the wind pulled the chute sideways, and I shouted "BRITISH!" again. As no one came I started to roll up my parachute when a farm labourer climbed over a nearby fence and requested confirmation that I was okay.

My 'shot off' leg was not, in fact, 'shot off'. It was just a tiny wound on my knee where a small piece of shrapnel had entered, and another the same size also half an inch away where it had come out. A lady with a horse then came along and I draped my parachute over the animal. Off we went on foot until a van took me to Lyme Regis Police Station. I was then entertained in the local pub whilst I awaited transport back to Warmwell. Someone from Air Sea Rescue arrived and I told him that I was pretty sure that 'my' *Heinkel* had gone into the drink.

Peter had probably been bounced by either an Me 109 or a 110; he never even saw the one that got him.

Flying Officer Peter Down about to take off in a 56 Squadron Hurricane during the Battle of Britain.

A week later, the Germans tried to hit Westlands again, this time with 20 Ju 88s of II/KG 51. Once more 56 Squadron joined the fray, and this time it was Sergeant Nichols' turn to meet the enemy. At 1530 hours, 'Nick' and four other Hurricanes were scrambled from Warmwell (from which forward airfield 56 operated on a daily basis): -

We took off in formation with me on the left of the leader, Flight Lieutenant Brooker, and I was 'Pip-squeak' man, my radio being blocked every 15 seconds. I can't remember hearing any R/T transmissions so perhaps the wireless was on the blink. I did not even hear the 'Tally ho!'. Flying in tight formation the first I saw was tracer coming from our leader's guns. Quick glimpse and I saw a Ju 88 and fired, still in formation, but had to break away to avoid collision with the Flight Lieutenant. I then lost the Squadron and pulled up, searching for the enemy. No sign of the bombers but 110s in a defensive spiral above. I pulled the 'tit' for maximum power and went to intercept.

A Spitfire was attacking the top of the spiral so I went head-on for the bottom. I fired but, perhaps not surprisingly in view of their heavy forward firing armament that I must have overlooked, was hit. Flames poured from the nose of my aircraft and the windscreen was black with oil, so I broke away as I could not see out. I turned the aircraft on its back to bale out at 25,000 feet. First time a slow roll but I remained seated. Second time I tumbled out, spinning. I told myself not to panic and gave the rip chord a steady pull. When the parachute deployed, the lanyards on one side were twisted. I tried to untangle them without success but relaxed, as at about 15,000 feet I appeared to be coming down reasonably slowly. I did not see the ground ultimately rush up at me and crumpled in a heap upon landing.

The Home Guard then appeared on the scene and told me to stick my hands up. They thought I was German but I just laughed at them between groans as I had actually broken my back. There was a Jerry parachutist stuck up a nearby tree, from the Ju 88, but the locals refused to get him down until they had seen to me.

Nick had landed near the village of Alton Pancras on the Dorset Downs. At about 1600 hours, Charlie Callaway, by coincidence another 19-year old, was ploughing in the 'Vernall' when he saw the Hurricane 'coming down hard and well on fire!' His younger brother Sam, 17, was rabbiting nearby and he too saw the doomed British fighter 'descending at a shallow angle but all ablaze and travelling sharpish like. It was so close that I could have reached out and touched it. There were several parachutes in the sky at the same time'. Nick's Hurricane, P3154, impacted at Austral Farm, some nine miles north of Dorchester.

Despite Nick's back injury, both he and Peter were lucky: both had met the enemy on their first operational patrol; both had been shot down but they had survived.

Later, Peter Fox also broke his back whilst serving with 56 Squadron, when he was 'flown into a haystack'. Recovered, he later went on to fly Spitfires with 234 Squadron, also out of Warmwell, until he was shot down by ground fire on October 20th, 1941, whilst crossing over the French coast near Cherbourg on a 'Rhubarb'. Fortunately Peter made a safe forced-landing and spent the remainder of the war in captivity. Unfortunately this mishap was the last in a string of events that prevented him from being commissioned, so it was with the rank of Warrant Officer that Peter ultimately left the RAF after the war.

Nick also recovered from his broken back and went back to operational flying. Instead of single-engine fighters, however, he found himself patrolling nocturnal skies over North Africa and later the Mediterranean in a 255 Squadron Bristol Beaufighter. He was not to meet the enemy again, but was more fortunate than Peter given that Nick was commissioned in March 1942. After the war he was seconded to BOAC, and upon release from the RAF in 1946, became an airline pilot with BEA. Nick flew throughout his working life, therefore, until eventually retiring to Worcestershire, where we met following an introduction from Ken Wilkinson during the early 1990s.

It was from talking to Nick that I first became particularly interested in the raids against Westlands on September 30th and October 7th, 1940. At the time I was actively involved in aviation archaeology, such as it is, and was obviously interested in investigating the crash site of his Hurricane. When I first explained our intention to Nick, his first reaction was "I threw it away in 1940 and I don't want it back now!" In time, however, he became increasingly interested in the project, to the extent that he accepted our invitation to join the (former) Malvern Spitfire Team for the excavation in November 1993.

Denis Nichols (centre), with members of the former Malvern Spitfire Team and eyewitnesses to his crash, at Austral Farm, Alton Pancras, Dorset, in November 1993. (Andrew Long)

Denis Nichols (left) stands on the crash site of his Hurricane with former German fighter pilot Hans 'Peter' Wulff. Sadly both are now deceased.

(Andrew Long)

Leutnant Hans Wulff poses in his Me 410, 1944.

Peter & Beryl Fox pictured with Hans 'Peter' Wulff, the cross-hedges remembered so vividly by Peter being directly behind them.

At Austral Farm we received a warm and kindly welcome from the Ralphs, and the villagers treated Nick like a king. He was both surprised and moved by this exhibition of respect and appreciation. We were not, however, the first enthusiasts to examine the site, at which comparatively little was left due to the nature of the crash. Many smashed components of the Hurricane were found, however, including a piece of armoured glass windscreen, through which Nick had last peered over 50 years before at the wrong end of an Me 110. Another Battle of Britain pilot, Squadron Leader Iain Hutchinson, who had flown Spitfires with 222 Squadron, and German veteran Hans 'Peter' Wulff joined us at the site. The latter was formerly a *Luftwaffe Leutnant* who had flown He 111s against the Russians, and Me 410s and FW 190s against the west until shot down and captured on Operation *Bodenplatte*, New Year's Day 1945. Peter had made his home in England after the war and was a true aviation enthusiast, having flown every year of his life, excepting only 1946, since learning to glide with the Hitler *Jugend*. It was tremendous that Peter was welcomed by the two British veterans, not as an enemy but as a fellow enthusiast and combat pilot who shared their common bond.

Peter Fox, left, discusses the finer points of his crash at Wootten Fitzpaine during the excavation of his Hurricane, November 1995.

Television cameras and reporters swarmed over the site, and with pilots and eyewitnesses present the events of October 7th, 1940, were vividly brought back to life as they all remembered that dramatic day. It was then that I decided to comprehensively research the events of September 30th and October 7th. Ken Wakefield had already published *Luftwaffe Encore*, concerning the West Country raids on September 25th & 27th, and old friend Dr Alfred Price had written about both August 18th (*The Hardest Day*) and September 15th (*Battle of Britain Day*). Producing a book about these other two hard-fought but lesser known days would fill a gap in existing literature, I thought, and so that proved to given the success of the work arising, *Angriff Westland* (Ramrod, 1994).

Peter Fox's story was not only included in *Angriff Westland* but also featured in *A Few of the Many* (Ramrod, 1995), in which I presented the stories of numerous pilot friends (similarly in fact to this book). It was not until November 1995, however, that we got around to returning Peter to his Wootten Fitzpaine crash site. The remains of his N2434 (US-H) was found exactly where Peter had described it, at the cross-hedges of four fields. Although smashed to pieces, many items were found, including eyelets from Peter's Sutton harness. At the site Peter and his wife Beryl, herself a wartime WAAF, were able to meet eyewitnesses who excitedly related their recollections, and rekindle acquaintance with the ever popular and gentlemanly Peter Wulff. Once more the excavation attracted much media interest, and was broadcast as a news item the length of Britain's south coast.

A gear from Peter Fox's Hurricane recovered during the 1980s by local enthusiast John Congram.

At the launch of *Angriff Westland*, which took place at Westland Helicopters in September 1994, we had presented Nick with a framed display of expertly conserved relics from his Hurricane. Peter Fox received a similar presentation at the launch of *Bader's Tangmere Spitfires* at Worcester Guildhall in October 1996. For Peter there was a bonus: having been made an honorary member of the Malvern Spitfire Team, we had applied to the MOD for ownership of N2434 to be transferred from the Crown to Peter himself. So it was that we were also able to pass Peter the official documentation confirming this to be the case, making him the only one of the Few to own his Battle of Britain aircraft!

The author presents Peter Fox with a display case featuring items from his Hurricane, ownership of which was transferred from the Crown to Peter himself. He is, therefore, the only Battle of Britain pilot to actually own his own fighter! *(Peter Nicholson)*

Unfortunately there is a sad postscript to this story. Firstly Peter Wulff died suddenly in 1997, and it was with great sadness that I spoke at his subsequent funeral service. Before he died, Peter gave me his *Legion Condor* cuff title, which I treasure to this day, and I still miss him greatly; it was such a rare bonus to have a fluently English speaking *Luftwaffe* veteran so very much on side. Secondly, Nick passed away in 2001. Shortly before his death, Ken Wilkinson had joined Nick on a holiday to Tenerife, from where these now ancient aviators sent us a postcard indicating that they were still enjoying high jinx!

Like Ken Wilkinson, Peter and Beryl Fox remain popular guests at our book launches and other events, Peter's sense of humour often having us all rolling in the aisles. There is no doubt that the man's great zest and love of life sustained him during his years behind the wire. Recently, Peter and Beryl became great-grandparents again, but after much deliberation decided against moving to be with their daughter in Cyprus. About that we could not, it must be said, be more pleased, as things would just not be the same around Ramrod without them.

Chapter Four

Sergeant Ken Wilkinson

Another personality with a sense of humour is Ken Wilkinson, who invariably answers the telephone "Frying tonight!" Here, he describes his personal route to the cockpit:-

Sitting in a classroom at school there was a tendency to take no notice of what gems of knowledge were being handed out, because it was far more important to be able to draw a recognisable side view of a fighter aircraft! It was Cheltenham Grammar School and there was plenty of opportunity because Gloster Aircraft was only a few miles away at Brockworth where Gamecocks and Gauntlets were being tested. There was also the Gloster entrant to the Schnieder Trophy, which, although it did not fly over Cheltenham, inspired us nonetheless and its outline was well known to us.

Then, when I was 17, my father asked if I would like to fly as a pilot in the RAF, to which there could only ever be one answer. Being a junior in an insurance office lost whatever minimal appeal it may previously have had. The application for a Short Service Commission went in when I was exactly 17¾ years of age and then my father said, "If you want to fly for a living then you'd better find out more about it". Five bobsworth with Alan Cobham's Flying Circus was not considered sufficient!

In April 1936, I went to Brockworth and was introduced to the test pilot 'Mr Summers' (now there's a name for you, he who first flew the Spitfire!) and put in the gunner's seat of a Hawker Hart Beeste, which was a variant produced for the South African Air Force. I was much too excited to worry about the seemingly inadequate clip that secured me to the seat, and don't think I really absorbed what was being told me about the parachute. I addressed Mr Summers as 'Sir' every time he spoke to me, clearly preparing myself for the deference to be paid to the officer set over me in the future.

The next half-hour was wonderful. Medium turns, steep turns, rolls, loops, dives etc and all looking backwards with no way of knowing what was coming next! Every pilot knows the feeling of bei9ng above the clouds for the first time – its even better looking backwards! When I was later given formal air experience on a Tiger Moth, I recall being somewhat blasé about it all.

After landing I expressed my gratitude in as profuse a manner as I could manage to Mr Summers and to my father who had arranged it. Afterwards it was back to being a junior in an insurance office with even less interest than before, having now had the great experience of flight in a fighting machine. There were those who had gone to great lengths to ensure that I got the experience, but I felt that inner superiority over those earthbound creatures who had not shared my experience.

Later on I discovered that none of Gloster Aircraft's employees ever volunteered for passenger duties and the test pilots did not like flying with a sack on the back seat, so I was actually helping them by taking the flight.

I did not, in fact, get a commission at that time, but joined the VR and

Pre-Fighter Course: Montrose, June 1940. Sergeants Nichols and Wilkinson at right, in that order, first row seated on bench, and Peter Fox fourth from right, same row.

learnt to fly at Staverton. On September 1st, 1939, I was called up, and completed my service flying training, with Denis Nichols and Peter Fox, between May and August 1940. Then it was off to 7 OTU, Hawarden and Spitfires, before joining 616 Squadron at Kirton.

616 Squadron was an auxiliary unit which had been heavily engaged during August 1940 whilst flying from Kenley (as described in the chapter concerning William Walker). Losses were extremely high, and when the Squadron was withdrawn on September 3rd, only eight of its original pilots had survived. After a brief spell at Coltishall, 616 settled in at Kirton where it became categorised a 'C' unit. On September 7th, Air Chief Marshal Dowding and other officers of Air rank held the 'Going downhill conference', so called because of the recognition of the fact that there were not enough combat ready replacement pilots. The OTUs were working flat out, but were still not producing enough pilots, in spite of all the short cuts. The solution arrived at by Air Chief Marshal Dowding and Air Vice-Marshal Park, the Commander-in-Chief of 11 Group, was to categorise fighter squadrons 'A', 'B' or 'C' units. 'A' were those in the front line and maintained with a minimum strength of 16 pilots, 'B' were those being rested but with a minimum of six combat ready pilots amongst the establishment of 16, and which could

be called upon if necessary. 'C' were those unlikely to be called into battle given that they were rebuilding to strength following losses suffered in the combat zone. The minimum number of combat ready pilots in a 'C' unit was three, and it was down to these men to pass on their experience to the new boys.

When Sergeant Wilkinson joined 616 Squadron, it was therefore being used as an extension of the OTU process, providing further training for a host of new pilots between the end of the actual OTU courses and a further posting to a squadron in the combat zone (as combat ready pilots). So it was that in October 1940, Ken moved on again, this time to fly Spitfires with 19 Squadron at Fowlmere:-

> When I arrived at Duxford there was a Hurricane beating the place up at very low level. I asked the guard who the pilot was, and without hesitation he said "Squadron Leader Bader". Of course I already knew of the great man by reputation, so thought 'Well, this is going to be interesting!'

> Squadron Leader Brian Lane DFC, who was very popular, commanded 19 Squadron, and as an NCO I got to know people like George Unwin and Harry Steere. They were professional, pre-war, airmen, and both were superb fighter pilots.

> Really, and probably fortunately for me upon reflection, I joined the Squadron a bit late on to see much action during the Battle of Britain, which was now coming to a close. Consequently I shot nothing down, but by the same token I did not get shot down myself, so I call it a 'no score draw'!

Early in 1941, Ken became an instructor at a Fighter Gunnery School, returning to operational flying in 1943, initially with 234 Squadron and subsequently with 165 Squadron. With these units Ken, who had by now been commissioned, flew the usual round of operational sorties. After that tour, Ken became an instructor, ending up at Honeybourne in Worcestershire. There he flew Hurricanes on fighter affiliation exercises with Wellingtons from the OTU based there. Being a Midlander himself, and now married with a baby on the way, the arrangement suited Ken perfectly.

The Three Musketeers! Ken Wilkinson, Peter Fox and Denis Nichols. Sadly, 'Nick' is now deceased.

After the war, Ken became a surveyor. Now retired, he lives with his daughter, Penny, in the West Midlands and enjoys his golf most weeks. He is also an enthusiastic member of both the Battle of Britain Fighter Association and the Spitfire Society, and thoroughly enjoys representing the Few at various air shows and other events. We have also been together several times to tell primary school children about the Battle of Britain, and Ken's relaxed and amusing manner always helps to get the point across in a way the children will remember and understand.

One thing I will always remember about Ken Wilkinson is an occasion during which we were filming with Keith Wilkinson (no relation) of Central TV News. Ken and fellow former Spitfire pilot Ron Rayner DFC were looking over a Merlin engine recovered from a Spitfire's crash site when suddenly Ken put his arm around Ron and said "As a Spitfire pilot, you were a cocky bugger, a cut above the rest, isn't that right, Ron old boy?" Some things, it seems and despite advancing years, never change!

Ken Wilkinson at a recent Ramrod book launch

(Andrew Long)

Chapter Five

Flight Sergeant George Unwin DFM & Bar

GeORGE Unwin will always be amongst Fighter Command's most outstanding pilots.

A Yorkshireman, George was the son of a miner and was a grammar school boy. In 1929, he joined the RAF as an apprentice clerk, but volunteered for aircrew in 1935. Selected for pilot training, he began learning to fly at Woodley before completing his service flying training at Wittering. He then joined 19 Squadron at Duxford.

At this time, 19 Squadron was equipped with the Gauntlet biplane fighter, but in August 1938 became the first squadron to receive the new Supermarine Spitfire. George Unwin was, in fact, the first RAF NCO pilot to ever fly a Spitfire. On March 9th, 1939, however, he found himself in trouble during a training flight in K9797:-

A coolant pipe had broken causing the engine to partially seize up. I decided to land on a large playing field, near Sudbury in Essex, and was doing fine, with undercarriage down, until the school children who were playing on the various pitches saw me descending (I was apparently on fire and trailing smoke). They ran towards me and on to the path I had selected for a landing. I was then less than 100 feet, so decided to stuff the Spitfire into the thick hawthorn hedge just in front of me. The impact broke my straps, and I gashed my right eyebrow on the windscreen but was otherwise unhurt. For this I received an Air Officer Commanding's commendation.

By September 1939, 19 Squadron was the most experienced Spitfire squadron in the RAF. In February the following year, the unit was joined by Flying Officer Douglas Bader who had lost both legs in a flying accident during 1931. Before then he had been a gifted sportsman and aerobatics pilot who had been a Cranwell chum of the Commanding Officer's, Squadron Leader Geoffrey Stephens. Regulations, however, prevented Bader from flying before the war, after he had mastered his artificial limbs and in spite of passing the necessary flying test. As a result he left the service in 1933, but upon declaration of war, as a trained pilot, was welcomed back into the fold. Much had changed during the time that he had been away, however, not least the aircraft. In Bader's pre-war days he had flown Bristol Bulldog biplane fighters with a fixed pitch propeller and fixed undercarriage. Now he was learning to fly the fast Spitfire monoplane, the airscrew of which (Mk IA) had a two-pitch setting, and retractable undercarriage. Changing pitch is similar to the effect of changing gear in a car, but on one occasion Bader attempted to take off in the wrong pitch, the result of which was him barely coming 'unstuck' and crashing into a dry stone wall! Ironically, his artificial legs were damaged beyond repair and so he received a replacement pair, as George remembers:-

Sometime after Bader's accident we were at Horsham St Faith's, to which we flew from Duxford every morning to be at Readiness for convoy patrols and the like. Whilst slumbering in the pilot's hut early one morning, Bader persisted in filing his new tin legs, to get them in perfect working order and fit, and so I remonstrated with him for this constant scratching and scraping whilst I was trying to sleep. At the time, the Walt Disney film 'Snow White & the Seven Dwarves' was very popular, and Bader replied "Oh shut up, Grumpy!", 'Grumpy' being one of the characters in the film. The name stuck, and from then on 'Grumpy' has been my nickname!

When the fighting started on the Continent in May 1940, Air Chief Marshal Dowding refused to send his precious Spitfires over the Channel. The Advanced Air Striking Force, already in France, was equipped with Hurricanes, which were more plentiful although slightly lacking in performance. As losses mounted, Hurricane squadrons flew from coastal bases like Hawkinge to operate in France on a daily basis. Every night they flew back to England, however, and so it went on. The Spitfire pilots were frustrated, but their Commander-in-Chief knew that if France fell, the Germans were likely to attack Britain with a view to mounting a seaborne invasion, and that being the case he would need all of his fighters, and Spitfires in particular, to defend these shores. To Air Chief Marshal Dowding, 'security of base' was the most important doctrine. At the time of Dunkirk, Spitfires did participate in the air operation in support of the evacuation. Although they operated little further than the French coast, for the first time the Spitfire clashed with the Me 109.

Squadron Leader Brian Lane DFC, the highly regarded 23-year old CO of 19 Squadron.

On May 26th, 1940, 19 Squadron experienced its first major combat of the war. Over Calais, Squadron Leader Stephenson led his Spitfires in a textbook formation attack on a group of *Stukas*. Flying along sedately, their speed matching that of their prey, the Spitfires made an easy target for the marauding and combat experienced Me 109s, which fell on 19 Squadron in a surprise attack. Within seconds two Spitfires were despatched from the fight: Squadron Leader Stephenson forced-landed on the nearby beach and was captured, and Pilot Officer Watson was killed. In a flash, the 109s were gone, leaving the Spitfire pilots shaken and confused. George Unwin:-

> The tacticians who wrote the book really believed that in the event of war it would be fighter versus bomber only. What they could not foresee was Hitler's modern ground tactics that would take his armies to the Channel ports in an unprecedented advance, thus providing bases for his fighters in the Pas-de-Calais and therefore putting London itself within their limited range. Our tight formations, which we practised extensively before the war, were actually useless in combat, what happened to Stephenson and Watson being a perfect example of just how flawed our fighter tactics were. Over Dunkirk, we had tried to put into practice years of peacetime training, based upon unrealistic perceptions, and paid a heavy price. Our formation attacks were perfectly impressive for the Hendon Air Pageant, but useless for modern air fighting which, after all, is for what they were intended.

The Spitfire squadrons had to learn fast, on the job, and indeed they did. By the end of Operation DYNAMO, Flight Sergeant Unwin had personally destroyed three enemy aircraft, plus a probable and a share in a probable He 111.

When the Battle of Britain started, so too began a frustrating time for the pilots of 12 Group, protecting the industrial Midlands and the north. The enemy's main thrust was against London and the Southeast, and targets along the south coast generally. These areas, however, were defended by 11 and 10 Groups. The Air-Officer-Commanding of 11 Group, Air Vice-Marshal Keith Park, understood perfectly the System and knew what was required of him. So as to preserve his fighters, he attacked using penny packet formations, as a result of which his pilots were always outnumbered. When 11 Group's airfields were threatened, however, and when his own fighters were in action further forward, Air

Vice-Marshal Park was entitled to call upon both 10 and 12 Groups to protect them. As we have already read previously in this book, for certain 12 Group personalities, including both the AOC and Acting Squadron Leader Douglas Bader, the CO of 242 Squadron, this lack of direct involvement was intolerable.

By mid-August, in spite of the heavy activity in the south east, 19 Squadron remained engaged upon providing protection to convoys moving along Britain's East Coast. At 1730 hours on August 16th, however, 'A' Flight, which was returning to Coltishall from such a patrol, was asked to investigate an incoming raid. George recalls the incident well:-

> We left Coltishall at 1715 and were ordered to 15,000 feet, which was altered to 12,000. After 20 minutes a large formation of enemy aircraft was spotted, bombers escorted by Me 110s at the rear and Me 109s above. As we went in to attack the bombers, the 110s saw us and attacked. I latched on to a 110 and gave him a short burst. He half-rolled and went down almost vertically. I could not see what had happened to him as I was attacked by another. I out-turned him and found myself with a perfect target at close range. My starboard cannon had a stoppage, but I fired the remainder of my port cannon's ammunition into the 110. Bits fell off the enemy aircraft and he went into a steep dive, during which the tail came off. I followed him down and when I came out of cloud I saw the end of a splash in the sea which I assume was him.

Other pilots, however, were frustrated. At this time 19 Squadron was equipped with the Spitfire Mk IB, which was armed with two 20mm cannons, as opposed to the usual battery of eight .303 Browning machine-guns. Before the war, the German designers had recognised the need for heavier armament for fighter aircraft than standard rifle calibre ammunition. Consequently the Me 109E was armed not only with two 7.92mm machine-guns, but also with two 20mm *Oerlikon* cannons. This gave the 109 a powerful punch indeed, and to put this into perspective bear in mind that a rifle calibre bullet is smaller than an adult's little finger, whilst a 20mm cannon shell is comparable in size to a clenched fist! Albeit late in the day, the RAF was desperate to give the Spitfire 20mm cannons. The problem, however, was that the Spitfire's thin wing section did not permit the available weapon, made by Hispano Suiza, to be mounted as intended. The cannon was fitted on its side, and an improvised chute constructed for the ejection of shell cases. Under stress and whilst in flight, however, the wing section flexed, resulting in the cannon jamming. As, unlike the 109, the Spitfire Mk IB was not armed with machine-guns as well, this meant that the pilot had no back up armament in the event of a stoppage. In combat this could prove extremely hazardous to say the least, and understandably the pilots were unhappy with this arrangement. On August 16th, several pilots experienced stoppages; had they not done so, the damage inflicted on the enemy would undoubtedly been greater. George:-

> The cannons were a real headache. We wanted and needed them, no doubt about that, but we didn't need the stoppages! Eventually the Commander-in-Chief himself, Air Chief Marshal Dowding, flew over to Fowlmere to talk to us about it and he listened carefully to what we had to say. Soon afterwards we were able to swap our Mk IBs with ordinary machine-gun armed Mk IAs, which came largely from an OTU.

Experiments were also in hand to produce a Spitfire with an appropriate mixture of both cannon and machine-gun armament, and towards the end of August 19 Squadron received X4231. This Spitfire had a 20mm cannon and two .303 machine-guns in each wing. Pilot Officer Arthur Vokes flew the aircraft on a number of trial flights at Sutton Bridge, and no problems were experienced. Unfortunately the aircraft was lost on August 31st, when Flying Officer James Coward was flying it when shot down over Royston. Nevertheless this combination of armament was considered correct, and the 'B' Wing was subsequently adopted. Ultimately the problems with mounting the cannon were solved by adding blisters to both the upper and lower wing surfaces, this permitting the cannon to be mounted as intended by the manufacturer, and accommodating the bulbous ammunition drum. It is largely thanks to the pioneering work by 19 Squadron in difficult conditions that these improvements were brought about.

Again as previously explained, after an engagement on August 30th, Squadron Leader Douglas Bader persuaded Air Vice-Marshal Leigh-Mallory to let him lead a three squadron strong 'Wing' of 12 Group fighters. So it was that 19 Squadron found itself being the Spitfire squadron assigned to this experiment. The intention was that the Hurricane squadrons, 242 and 310, would operate out of Duxford, whilst the Spitfires, based a short distance away at Fowlmere but with their superior performance, would operate as top cover. Contrary to some claims, there was no time lost to forming up, Squadron Leader Bader just set course and everyone did their best to follow him, despite the differences in individual aircraft performance. On September 7th, when the Germans began pounding London for the first time, Squadron Leader Bader led his formation into action for the first time. Although at a tactical disadvantage due to having been caught on the climb, battle was joined. Amongst the successful RAF pilots was Flight Sergeant Unwin.

Having initially attacked an Me 110, 'Grumpy' found himself alone at 4,000 feet. Climbing to 25,000, he saw a 'Hurricane squadron going somewhere in a hurry' and followed them. Suddenly three separate enemy formations comprising 30 bombers each, with their inevitable fighter escort, appeared. As the Hurricanes attacked the bombers, George found himself surrounded by Me 109s; fighting a running battle between Ramsgate and west London, he remembers:-

> The usual fight ensued during which I definitely hit at least five of them but only two were shot down, both in flames. I then climbed for a breather and shadowed the third enemy formation when I saw yet a fourth arriving. By this time two of the other three formations had turned north and the other went straight on in a westerly direction. The leading formation turned east and I was at 25,000' and above them. As there did not seem to be any of their escorts left, I dived on the rear vic and gave them the rest of my ammunition, about 50 rounds in each gun, and from 450, closing to 50 yards range. The bomber at which I fired wobbled a bit but otherwise carried on. Without ammunition, I then returned to Fowlmere.

Without crash locations, it is difficult to ascertain which Me 109s were destroyed by Flight Sergeant Unwin, although two of the three machines lost over England that afternoon by JG51 appear most likely.

By the end of the day, 1,800 Londoners were dead or seriously injured. For Air Vice-Marshal Park this change in targets from his airfields to the capital was a miracle:-

It was burning all down the river. It was a horrid sight. But I looked down and said "Thank God for that", because I knew that the Nazis had switched their attack from our fighter stations thinking that they were knocked out. They weren't, but they were pretty groggy.

Some 19 Squadron pilots at Fowlmere during the Battle of Britain. From left to right: Squadron Leader Brian Lane, Sergeant Jack Potter (POW), Sergeant Bernard 'Jimmy' Jennings DFM, Flight Sergeant George 'Grumpy' Unwin DFM, Pilot Officer Ray Aeberhardt (KIA, 1940), Flight Sergeant Harry Steere (KIA, 1944), Flying Officer Frank Brinsden (NZ, POW), Flight Lieutenant Walter 'Farmer' Lawson DFC (MIA, 1941), Pilot Officer Alan 'Ace' Haines DFC (Killed in flying accident), Pilot Officer Arthur Vokes (killed in flying accident), Flight Lieutenant Wilf Clouston (POW), Flying Officer Hugh Thomas.

The attacks on London continued relentlessly, day and night. On September 11th, the 'Big Wing' was back in action, as George recalled for me nearly 50 years later:-

I attacked a Dornier over London but was stupid enough to be shot down by the gunner they carried in a dustbin below the fuselage. I landed in a field near Brentwood in Essex and was taken to RAF North

Weald by the army. With the aid of a fitter plus spares, 'QV-H' was repaired and I flew it back to Duxford two days later. One bullet had penetrated the armoured windscreen, however, so as this could not be repaired on station P9546 was then flown away to a Maintenance Unit. This Spitfire was one of those replacements for the Mk IBs that we received from the OTUs.

His forced-landing was much commended in the 19 Squadron ORB:-

Flight Sergeant Unwin made a wizard forced-landing with undercarriage down!!!!

On September 15th, Flight Sergeant Unwin enjoyed considerable success. Some of 19 Squadron's Spitfires managed to engage the 109s, as had been planned; at 1210, over Westerham, Kent, George engaged 3/JG 53's *Staffelkapitän, Oberleutnant* Haase, in a dogfight:-

I was Red Three with Flight Lieutenant Lawson. We sighted the enemy aircraft that were flying in vics of three. The escorts dived singly onto us and I engaged and Me 109 with a yellow nose. I gave one burst of six seconds and it burst into flames. The pilot baled out and the enemy aircraft crashed between Redhill and Westerham.

Haase was killed as his parachute failed to open.

Flight Sergeant Unwin and his beloved dog, 'Flash'.

During the next sortie that day, 'Grumpy' was Lane's Red 3 and reported sighting 'thousands of 109s'. When the Wing was attacked, at close range 'Grumpy' fired a three-second burst at a 109, which half-rolled and dived steeply into the clouds. Although the Spitfire pilot pursued his prey, he lost the 109 at 6,000 feet when his windscreen froze up. Climbing back up to 25,000, a *Rotte* of 109s appeared above him, flying south. Flight Sergeant Unwin gave chase and caught both over Lydd. The first burst into flames and went down vertically, the second crashed into the sea. It is likely that these two 109s were from I/JG 77: *Oberleutnant* Kunze, of the *Geschwaderstabschwarm*, who was killed when his aircraft crashed at Lympne, as was *Unteroffizier* Meixner who crashed into the sea off Dungeness at about 1455. This brought Flight Sergeant Unwin's total of Me 109s definitely destroyed this day to three.

September 17th saw the awards two gallantry decorations awarded to the Duxford squadrons: 310's Flight Lieutenant Jeffries received the DFC, and 19's Flight Sergeant George Unwin the DFM, his squadron's ORB commenting:-

Good show! Ten certain Huns to his credit.

The majority of George Unwin's claims can be verified today and there can be no doubt that this award was much deserved. 'Grumpy' was undoubtedly amongst the most experienced Spitfire pilots in the RAF at this time.

On September 18th, George destroyed an Me 110, and on September 27th another 109. The latter combat was a protracted dogfight lasting some 10 minutes, and which took the Spitfire pilot dangerously near the French coast. Eventually George fired a 30° deflection shot. The 109 stalled and span into the sea.

Although British official sources consider that the Battle of Britain concluded on October 31st, the fact is that there are other dates apparently more appropriate. September 15th, which was a decisive day as any and now celebrated annually as 'Battle of Britain Day', or September 30th, on which day the Germans conceded that they were unable to further sustain such heavy losses to its bomber force, are just two dates that spring readily to mind. Whatever, despite October 31st being chosen by the authorities, the fighter forces continued to clash over the south coast until early 1941.

On November 5th, 1940, Flight Sergeant Unwin destroyed another Me 109, shared a 110 on November 15th, and a 109 on November 28th. By this time he was in Fighter Command's list of successful pilots, and on December 6th a Bar to his DFM was gazetted. Later that month he was rested and left 19 Squadron to attend an instructor's course at Cranwell. All of this is remarkable considering that George joined the RAF as an airman, and during the Battle of Britain was 27-years old, much older than fighter pilot's average age.

George gives his views at the end of the Battle of Britain:-

> At the time I felt as though nothing out of the ordinary was happening. I had been trained for the job and fortunately already had a lot of flying experience. I was always most disappointed if the Squadron got into a scrap when I was off duty, and this applied to all of the pilots I knew. It was only after the event that I began to realise how serious defeat would have been, but we had never considered the prospect of defeat, it just wasn't possible in our eyes. That was simply our outlook at the time. As we lost pilots and aircraft, replacements were always forthcoming. Of course our new pilots were inexperienced, but so were the German replacements. It was clear at the end of 1940 that these pilots had not the stomach for a scrap with a Spitfire!

After such a successful time in 1940, and considering his age, many would consider that they had done enough. Indeed, there were a small number of pilots who disappeared into Training Command after their first operational tours, never to reappear on the front line scene. For both George Unwin and his 19 Squadron friend Harry Steere, however, such a prospect was intolerable. The pair made real fuss to get back on 'ops'. The slightly younger Steere achieved this in 1943, going to fly Mosquito Pathfinders, and George and finally achieved his goal in April 1944, by threatening to transfer to Bomber Command! George then went to fly Mosquitoes too, but on night intruder operations with 613 Squadron. By then, however, Flight Lieutenant Harry Steere DFC DFM was dead, having been shot down over Rennes just three days after D-Day.

By VE Day, 'Grumpy' was Flight Lieutenant and there followed a series of instructing and staff appointments until his promotion to Squadron Leader in 1947, at which time he was posted overseas. Commanding 84 Squadron and flying Bristol Brigands, he flew operations during the Malayan Emergency, for service during which he received the DSO.

The author and Wing Commander George Unwin DSO DFM* RAF (Ret'd) at the launch of Through Peril to the Stars, *Great Malvern, 1993.*

Wing Commander GC Unwin DSO DFM & Bar retired from the RAF in January 1961, eight months before I was born. Despite the great difference between our ages, George and I have enjoyed a great friendship for nearly 20 years, since I first contacted him in connection with research for my first book, Spitfire Squadron (Air Research Publications, 1990). We enjoyed both protracted correspondence and numerous meetings at George's south coast bungalow. Those occasions were really inspirational, and I always opened George's letters with anticipation, knowing that they would be full of information.

The puzzling thing for me at that time was how here we had a very successful Battle of Britain pilot, whose claims actually tallied with

German losses, but about whom so little had been written. True, George had not sought or wanted recognition, but it seems a great pity that, although in the years since our first meeting a number of authors have now followed our lead and written about him, George never wrote his own memoirs. Now that would have been a document worth recording, extending as it did from the pre-war regular RAF to post war action in Malaya. To say that significant changes and events took place between those times would be an understatement, and George was a participant in some and eyewitness to others. This man was a true professional and an aggressive, gifted fighter pilot, make no mistake.

When *Spitfire Squadron* was launched at the RAF Battle of Britain Museum, Hendon, it was a real honour that every 19 Squadron Battle of Britain pilot resident in the UK joined us for the signing. It is a sad fact, however, that 12 years later a number are now deceased, although George, aged 87, is still with us. Long may he remain so!

Wing Commanders George Unwin and Bernard 'Jimmy' Jennings, who were great friends in 19 Squadron during the Battle of Britain, at an early Ramrod book launch. Sadly 'Jimmy' is now deceased.

Chapter Six

Sergeant 'Mike' Bush

On August 20th, 1939, Basil Martin 'Mike' Bush joined the RAFVR at Cambridge. From September 1st – October 26th he completed his 'square bashing' at No 1 Initial Training Wing, Cambridge, where he was billeted at St John's College. Thence he proceeded to No 6 Elementary Flying Training School at Sywell, where he completed his *ab initio* instruction. After service flying training on Masters at Montrose, it was south to No 7 OTU, Hawarden, to fly Harvards and 'Hurricanes at last!' On July 16th, 1940, Sergeant Bush was posted to 504 'City of Nottingham' Squadron, a Hurricane squadron of the Auxiliary Air Force. He joined the Squadron at Castletown in Scotland, and flew south to Hendon with the unit on September 5th.

Awaiting the call to scramble, Mike recalls that appropriately the pilots' favourite tune was Vera Lynn's 'Room Five Hundred & Four'. On September 7th, 504 was amongst the squadrons scrambled in response to the major attack on London. Over the Thames Estuary, Mike's Hurricane, P3021, 'TM-N', was shot up by a 109. A cannon shell passed through his instrument panel and into the reserve petrol tank beyond:-

> I was damned lucky not to catch fire as when hit the petrol splashed all over me! Fortunately it did not ignite and I managed a safe forced-

landing on the Isle of Sheppey. It was a bit hairy for a moment or two, though! Due to repairs being carried out I was unable to return to Hendon with my aircraft until September 9th. They gave me a week off to recover, so I did not fly again until September 17th.

On September 25th, the *Luftwaffe* mounted a successful raid on the Bristol Aircraft Company at Filton, near Bristol. As there were several other important targets in the West Country connected with the aircraft industry, and in anticipation of further attacks, the decision was made to move 504 Squadron from Hendon to Filton. The Squadron moved there the following day, which proved a wise move as on September 27th, the Germans returned. On that occasion the target was Parnall Aircraft at Yate, only this time the enemy was harshly treated by 10 Group, including 504. On September 30th, KG 55 intended to smash Westland Aircraft at Yeovil but due to cloud covering the target bombed the neighbouring town of Sherborne by mistake. In what was the last truly great daylight battle of 1940, 504 Squadron's Hurricanes were scrambled from Filton and pursued the retreating *Heinkels* until dangerously close to the Cherbourg peninsula. Sergeant Jones shot down two He 111s, and Sergeant Bush damaged another, as did several other pilots:-

After the interception I was unable to make radio contact with Filton. As it was getting dark and I was lost somewhere south of Bristol I was fearful of getting caught up in balloon cables, so I decided to land in a field. I picked what I thought to be a long landing run in a particular field which I had spotted, but on the approach I came in low over a hedge and landed, only to discover that it was a much shorter field than the one I had selected and saw a brick wall ahead! Having touched down I could do nothing else but jam on my brakes and switch off the engine. This resulted in tipping the Hurricane up onto its nose. It then flipped over onto its back and I was left hanging by my harness upside down and several feet from the ground. Thankfully I was soon rescued by Observer Corps personnel from nearby Priddy village. By coincidence, the aircraft concerned was P3021, in which I had been shot down over the Thames.

At that juncture, P3021 and Mike Bush parted company, as the aircraft was taken away to a repair depot. The Hurricane was to have further adventures with other pilots before finally crashing and being written off over a year later.

Hawker Hurricane P3021, of 504 Squadron and pictured at Filton in the Battle of Britain, which Sergeant Bush crashed twice!

On December 17th, 1941, 504 Squadron moved from Filton to Exeter, also in 10 Group, where it was joined later by the Spitfires of 66 Squadron. During that period, Mike often flew nocturnal patrols:-

> We were sent up to take over from the AA at Plymouth during a raid on February 10th, 1941. The guns were supposed to stop firing and let us have a go, but they kept on, apparently uncaring as to who got hit. We soon got fed up with this and returned to base, however!

Mike was commissioned later that year, and went to fly Hurricanes in Russia. After that tour he became an instructor prior to converting Mosquito bombers. Flying with 139 Squadron at Upwood, Mike flew 54 operational trips, 18 of which were to Berlin, the 'Big City', itself. A tour was actually considered complete at 30 trips, so Mike's DFC was clearly much deserved.

After the war, Mike returned to banking and eventually retired with his wife, Irene, to a tranquil spot in Lincolnshire. Although a member of the Battle of Britain Fighter Association, Flight Lieutenant BM 'Mike' Bush DFC has all but faded into obscurity.

> I was just doing my job, along with countless others. I certainly do not consider that I did anything special, far from it.

Typically modest, Mike Bush is a real gentleman. It is hard to relate this white-haired elderly citizen, who now cares for Irene, to the Battle of Britain and Bomber Command veteran that he is. Personally I think that Mike is a special person, a very special person indeed.

'Mike' Bush pictured at home in 1994
(*Mark Postlethwaite*)

Sadly 'Mike' passed away after this book was written, in July 2002, aged 88.

Chapter Seven

Pilot Officer William Walker

William Walker is another of life's true gentlemen, and has not only been a most welcome guest at many book launches but also an entertaining dinner companion. Now aged 89, it is a long time since he joined the RAFVR in 1938! At the time, William was working for Halls Oxford Brewery and attached to Kidlington aerodrome for flying lessons. When called up on September 1st, 1939, Sergeant

Walker had completed sufficient flying hours for his elementary training to be considered complete. He therefore went straight to ITW Cambridge, and afterwards to Brize Norton where he was converted to Harvards. There, however, William had the most incredible escape when he walked away, virtually unscathed, from an absolutely horrendous night landing accident. Indeed, having staggered from the crash site across several fields, when he walked into the Mess his fellow students assumed that they were looking at a ghost! As William later said 'Whilst at Kidlington they had 26 student pilots, and I was No 26. My instructor said that being twice 13 it was a lucky number; having escaped the Harvard crash I was inclined to agree!'

In April 1940, William received not only his coveted pilot's flying brevet but also a commission. On June 18th, he joined 616 'South Yorkshire' Squadron of the Auxiliary Air Force, based at Leconfield:-

> The early days of war were interesting in so far as we were so unprepared for what was to come. It is my lasting regret that I did not have more operational training – trying to pick it up with the Squadron straight from flying school was a pretty haphazard affair. For instance, I flew my first Spitfire on June 23rd, and was declared operational on July 1st.

Flying from Leconfield, 616 Squadron was involved in the 'Junkers Party', the action fought off the northeast coast on August 15th. On that occasion the Germans had not expected to find Spitfires and Hurricanes so far north, wrongly believing that all available single-engine fighters must have already been committed to battle in the south. From the aerodromes in Norway from whence these raiders came, England lay beyond the range of the Me 109, so consequently escort was provided by Me 110s. The latter proved inadequate to the task, however, and the Germans took a beating, so much so, in fact, that the *Luftwaffe* never again tried to attack the north in daylight. 616 Squadron engaged 50 bombers and a gaggle of 110s at 15,000 feet, 10 miles off Flamborough Head. Subsequently, eight bombers were claimed as destroyed, four probably destroyed and two damaged, all for no loss. The absence of Me 109s, however, gave the inexperienced defenders a false impression of air fighting. This was soon to change, drastically.

On August 19th, 616 Squadron flew south to Kenley Sector Station, in 11 Group. Only the previous day, Kenley had been hit hard, and so the Station bore little resemblance to the formal and orderly environment left behind by 616 at Leconfield, as William remembers:-

> The Mess at Kenley was a rather sombre building and far removed from the modern, light and cheerful Mess at Leconfield. Kenley bore many scars as witness to damage and loss of life caused by enemy action. An atmosphere of purpose prevailed and we found ourselves having to respond to a life of far greater activity than at Leconfield where only a few minor raids had disrupted our existence.

Three days later the Squadron experienced its first clash with the enemy whilst operating from Kenley: Green Section was bounced over Dover by a *Staffel* of JG 51's Me 109s. Within seconds Pilot Officer Hugh 'Cocky' Dundas was taking to his parachute, his Spitfire in flames, and a cannon shell damaged Pilot Officer Lionel 'Buck' Casson's fighter. Sergeant Wareing, however, claimed a 109 destroyed in the resulting skirmish.

On August 25th, 616 Squadron was vectored to intercept a raid comprising 20 Do 17s escorted by a *Gruppe* of Me 109s. Before reaching the bombers, the Spitfires were bounced and broken up by the 109s. Sergeant Westmoreland was killed and Sergeant Wareing was 'Missing' (later reported as a prisoner). In response, the Auxiliaries claimed two enemy aircraft destroyed and a probable.

William Walker:-

> We were very unsure of ourselves at this time. Everything happened so quick, and of course our formations of vics and lines astern were all wrong. There was so little information available to us. Very little was passed on by those squadrons that were relieved as they just couldn't wait to get the hell out of the place! Fighting in the south, where the 109s always seemed to have the advantage of height and sun, was very different indeed to chasing after unescorted bombers up north.

That having been said, 616 Squadron's initiation was not as brutal as experienced by some unfortunate squadrons. Studying the casualty lists, every now and again a squadron suddenly appears and suffers a far greater number of losses than the average. Inevitably, if one delves a little deeper, this invariably occurred when the squadron in question met Me 109s in strength for the first time and can only be described as traumatic.

August 26th, 1940, is a day that William Walker will always remember:-

> It was still dark when the Orderly awoke me with a cup of tea at 0330 that morning, just two days after my 27th birthday, which had passed unnoticed amid the current level of activity and excitement. I drank my tea slowly and gradually awakened to another day. It seemed such a short while since we had been 'stood down' the previous evening at about 2100 hours, and after which a few beers refreshed our spirits

before bed. However, I dressed and went down to breakfast, always a quiescent occasion at the unearthly hour of 0400! The sound of aero engines could be heard in the distance, indicating that the groundcrews were already busy. One was so accustomed to the drone of engines that it passed almost unnoticed amid the clatter of cups and plates.

Following breakfast I joined other pilots outside the Mess. We all climbed aboard a lorry and were driven to dispersal, to remain at 'Readiness', where a hut and a few tents constituted the Squadron's base. A few days earlier the Duke of Kent had actually paid us a visit at our modest location to wish us well.

That day I was allocated Spitfire R6633, and was to fly in Yellow Section led by Flying Officer Teddy St Aubyn, a former Guards officer. The plane stood within 50 yards of our hut and so I walked over and placed my parachute in the cockpit with the straps spread apart and ready for wearing immediately I jumped in. Two of the groundcrew stood by the plane with the starter battery plugged in. I walked back to the hut as the sun rose and added a little warmth to a chilly start. Pilots sat about either reading or exchanging the usual banter that had become routine. We had spent many months in this way, which was now a way of life. At 8 a.m. our second breakfast arrived at dispersal, and was just as fulfilling as our breakfast of four hours earlier: coffee, eggs, bacon, sausages and toast to replenish our undiminished appetites.

The telephone suddenly rang in the dispersal hut, and a shout went up of "Yellow Section Scramble! Patrol Dugneness/Dover Angels 20!". This sent me running for my Spitfire. I leapt on to the wing and was in the cockpit, parachute strapped on, within seconds. I pressed the starter and the engine fired immediately. The groundcrew removed the plug from the cowling and pulled the remote starter battery clear. I waved the chocks away and taxied the aircraft, following my Section Leader and Sergeant Ridley to the end of the runway for take off. Within minutes, Yellow Section was airborne. We headed east, climbing quickly and passing through cloud, reached our patrol course in some 15-20 minutes. We flew in a wide formation that day, in fact, and had been airborne for about an hour without sighting an enemy aircraft when suddenly several Me 109s appeared.

High above and unseen by Yellow Section, however, was the entire JG 51 (about 100 Me 109s), led in person by the *Kommodore*, Major Werner Mölders (the so-called 'Father of Modern Air Fighting' himself) on a *geschwader* strength *Freie Hunt.* Dropping behind and below the Spitfires, Mölders selected William Walker's Spitfire and attacked from the blind spot:-

When the 109s hit us I banked sharply to port, towards a 109, but suddenly my machine was raked with bullets. The one that attacked me did so from below and behind, I never even saw it. The flying controls ceased to respond and a sudden pain in my leg indicated that I had been hit. Baling out seemed to be a sensible option. My two comrades, St Aubyn and Ridley, had both vanished.

I pulled back the hood and tried to stand up but realised that I had not disconnected the radio lead, which was still plugged in, and had to remove my helmet before I was free to jump. The aircraft was still banking to port, so jumping out was easy, I was still at 20,000 feet and pulled the ripcord immediately. A sudden jerk indicated that all was well and that I was on my way down. I looked around but could not see a single aircraft. Below there was 10/10ths cloud. I had no idea where I was. It seemed to take ages to reach the clouds and passing through I realised that I was still over the Channel. Thinking that I would soon land in the sea prompted the thought that I had better remove my heavy flying boots. I did this and let them fall. I watched them spiral down for what seemed like ages and then realised that I was much higher than I thought. I inflated my Mae West and eventually landed in the sea. I easily discarded my parachute and could see the wreck of a ship sticking out of the water a few hundred yards away and swam to it. I reached it and climbed on, sitting there for about half an hour until a fishing boat came alongside and I clambered aboard. I was now extremely cold from my immersion and wet clothes.

The fishermen gave me a cup of tea, well laced with whisky, as we headed for land. When about two miles offshore, an RAF launch came alongside and I was transferred to it. By this time the tea concoction had worked quite disastrously on my cold stomach. Fortunately there was a loo aboard to which I retired with some relief. I was still enthroned when we reached Ramsgate harbour. An aircraftman kept knocking on the door and enquiring whether I was all right. It was some time before I was able to emerge! I as carried up the steps to a waiting ambulance, by which time quite a crowd had gathered and gave me a cheer as I was put in the ambulance. A kind old lady handed me a packet of cigarettes, so I decided that being shot down was perhaps not such a bad thing after all!

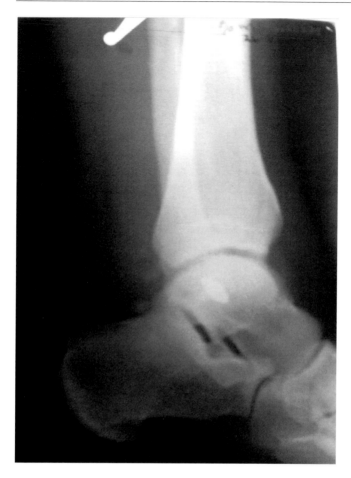

An X-Ray showing the German bullet lodged in William's foot.

Yellow Section's Sergeant Marmaduke Ridley had not been so lucky, however: he was dead, having been shot down by *Hauptmann* 'Joschko' Fözoe, *Staffelkapitän* of 4/JG 51. Yellow One, Flying Officer St Aubyn, had been shot down by *Oberleutnant* 'Pips' Priller, *Staffelkapitän* of 6/JG 51. The Spitfire caught fire but the wounded pilot managed to crash-land at Eastchurch. 616 Squadron also suffered other losses, including the death of Pilot Officer Moberley and another pilot wounded. William Walker summarises the day's events as 'traumatic'. More accurately for the Squadron as a whole, they could be described as 'catastrophic'. Since having arrived at Kenley a week previously, seven Spitfires lost, four pilots wounded and four killed; the squadron's clerk, clearly a master of the understatement, had recorded the action as 'a very unfortunate engagement'. The following day, whilst in transit between Ramsgate Hospital and RAF Hospital Halton, William Walker stopped off at Kenley to collect his belongings:-

> Whilst there I asked my driver to take me to dispersal so that I could say farewell to any remaining pilots. It proved a sad occasion, however, as the squadron had suffered severe losses and very few pilots actually remained operational.

> It was almost 2200 hours when we arrived at Halton RAF Hospital, where I was put to bed. Unfortunately, by this late hour, the kitchens had been closed for some hours but a wonderful night nurse produced an equally wonderful and indeed appropriate meal: scrambled eggs!

> After breakfast the following morning, doctors appeared and attended to the officers in my large ward of some 20 beds. Nobody came to see me, however, and apart from getting rather painful, I was beginning to worry about gangrene. The previous 48 hours had been somewhat traumatic to say the least, so my concern was not entirely unjustified!

> At noon the head doctor, a group captain, did his rounds. As he passed my bed he asked what I was in for. I told him that I had a bullet in my leg. He said "Oh yes, and who is looking after you?" When I told him that I had yet to see a doctor despite having arrived the previous night I thought that he was going to have a convulsion! He literally exploded and his wrath remains a vivid memory. Never were so many doctors torn off a bigger strip. It was action stations from then on, and within just 10 minutes I was in the operating theatre.

> When I regained consciousness, the surgeon was by my bedside. He said "I think you may like to have this", and handed me an armour-piercing bullet. He then told me that as he was prising open the bone in my leg to extract the bullet it shot out and hit the ceiling of the operating theatre! I still possess it today as a cherished souvenir.

> Fortunately my sense of humour never quite left me, and when a doctor later asked how my accident happened I assured him that I was not the victim of an accident, but of a determined attempt on my life by a German fighter pilot!

On August 26th, 616 Squadron had lost seven of the 12 Spitfires flown on operations that day; two pilots were dead and four more wounded. William Walker was one of the lucky ones. The Squadron's Orderly Clerk, clearly a master of the understatement, recorded that it had been 'a very unfortunate engagement'.

On September 3rd, 616 Squadron, comprising just eight of its original members who arrived at Kenley on August 19th, was relieved at Kenley by 64 Squadron. In those 15 days, 616 had lost a total of 11 Spitfires destroyed and three damaged. Five pilots had been killed, six wounded and one captured. In response, the Squadron claimed the destruction of 10 enemy aircraft destroyed, three probably destroyed, and six damaged. Of this 'bag', seven destroyed, two probables and three damaged were claimed by one man: Flight Lieutenant Denys Gillam AFC. For this feat he later received recognition by way of a DFC.

William Walker, his leg in plaster, was sent to complete his treatment at the Palace Hotel, Torquay, which had been converted into an RAF Hospital. Another patient there at the time was Flight Lieutenant James Brindley Nicholson, as William remembers:-

> A telegram arrived for him. 'Nick's' response was simply "Well, what d'you make of that?" He was genuinely puzzled, and not a little embarrassed, that of hundreds of brave deeds performed by RAF fighter pilots that summer, his had been singled out for this very great honour. His was the only Fighter Command VC because due to the speed of fighter combat it is difficult to find witnesses, supporting evidence being a pre-requisite. At first 'Nick' got into trouble for being improperly dressed because he refused to stitch the maroon ribbon onto his tunic. In the end I think he adopted the attitude that he was accepting the medal on behalf of us all. He was a good sport, in fact, and we enjoyed playing together in a four-piece band that we formed with other wounded pilots down at Torquay.

> On May 1st, 1941, I was considered fit enough to return to operations, so I re-joined 616 Squadron, which was then a part of Wing Commander Douglas Bader's Wing at Tangmere and was much changed. When I reported to the Wing Leader he tore me off a strip for being so careless as to have been shot down, which I thought was a bit off, to say the least. Suffice to say that I did not take to him, and he not to me, so three weeks later I was posted to an Aircraft Delivery Flight at Hendon. Later that summer, of course, it was announced that Douglas Bader himself had been shot down and captured by the Germans!

The rest of William's war was 'enjoyable but mundane', but on May 8th, 1945, he was able to call himself a survivor:-

The band in action at Torquay: Flight Lieutenant JB Nicholson VC at the mike, Pilot Officer William Walker provides percussion!

Looking back after all these years to the time when so many of us on Course 45 had such high hopes and felt invulnerable, it is terribly sad that some would not survive the year, would never even see the enemy, all of their hard work and training proving fruitless. Whilst they were just casualty statistics in the official records, to me they are a reminder of many happy days of friendship that are still well worth recalling and should be remembered.

They were the most exhilarating days, but one lost so many friends who were al so young. It is sad that the best pilots seemed to get killed whilst the 'hams' like me survived.

William Walker poses with the bullet extracted from his foot - over 60 years later at a Ramrod book launch

(Andrew Long)

Chapter Eight

Pilot Officer Richard Jones

Richard Jones was another VR pilot who had learned to fly at Woodley, near Reading. There he flew Harts, Hind and Audax biplanes before progressing to the Magister monoplane. Mobilised on September 1st, 1939, Richard's advanced service flying training was undertaken on Harvards at RAF Ternhill, in Shropshire. He was then taught how to fly Spitfires at No 5 OTU, Aston Down (near Stroud in Gloucestershire). In July 1940, Pilot Officer Jones was posted to fly Spitfires with 64 Squadron at Kenley:-

> Upon arrival at Kenley, I remember being met by the CO, an absolutely charming man and a real gentleman in every sense of the word, Squadron Leader ARD 'Don' MacDonell. He immediately made us new pilots feel at home, he called us his 'chicks'. We would find our CO a quiet but determined leader and an excellent fighter pilot. He looked after the best interests of all who served under him and he had the respect of all.

> To give us battle experience as quickly as possible whenever the time

allowed, we were paired off with a senior battle-experienced pilot to practise dog-fighting and yet more dog-fighting to give us both experience and confidence in the Spitfire and combat conditions. We were lucky to have that extra curricular training, which would have been impossible had we been posed to 64 later on that summer and for obvious reasons.

The operational focal point of every squadron was dispersal, which was a hut containing 12 beds, and an Orderly Clerk with a telephone. I well recall the three states of Readiness. The first was 'Readiness', which meant all pilots kitted up and ready to go. The next was at '15 minutes', which meant that you had to be in the Mess and available to be ready for flight in 15 minutes. Finally, '30 minutes', which meant that you could relax a bit, play billiards or go to the local cinema. From that state you could be called to '15 minutes' and so on.

64 Squadron outside the Mess at RAF Kenley during the Battle of Britain. Squadron Leader Don MacDonnell DFC at seventh from right, Pilot Officer Jones fifth from right.

If you were on Readiness, then that day you would rise very early, at around 4 a.m., so that you were at the aerodrome and ready before dawn in the event of an emergency. Immediately, you would be served a remarkable breakfast and the attention that we received from staff was amazing. After breakfast we used to get into what we called the 'Cattle Truck' to be driven over to Dispersal. We would then get kitted up, excepting our helmets and parachutes, which were placed on or in the aircraft, also at the ready, and waited in the Crew Room for something to happen. If you were not down on the board to fly, then it was a long day, waiting around. Most pilots spent their waiting time playing cards, chess, reading or sleeping. Suddenly the tranquillity would be shattered by the telephone's bell, Immediately everyone was tense, in anticipating of orders to scramble. Certainly the telephone stirred our senses quicker than anything else that I have ever experienced.

If it was a scramble, we ran to and got into our Spitfires, engines started and away. We would be given immediate instructions, such as 'Scramble Angels 10 over Dungeness'. We knew that because our radar based system of early warning, wherever we were sent there was always a good chance of meeting the enemy. If we did meet the Germans then of course we would engage them to the best of our ability.

When we came back, anybody who had been successful, perhaps in shooting down an enemy aircraft, might do such a thing as a 'victory roll', but those were not encouraged because it was not always known whether one's own aircraft was in fact damaged. Immediately upon landing the Intelligence Officer would take full details from each pilots of what had happened, whilst the groundcrew prepared the aircraft for immediate take-off. We then started the waiting process all over again, until such time as we were either scrambled again or relieved of Readiness by another squadron. We would then drop back to 15 minutes, then 30 minutes, and so the cycle went on. In fairness despite the actual state of Readiness, we were always pretty much ready for most eventualities.

One incident of many that I can still recall was when we of 64 Squadron were visited by the Air Minister, Sir Archibald Sinclair. We were all lined up to meet him, standing in front of our Spitfires. He congratulated us on the work that we were doing and in his opening words thanked us as *Hurricane* pilots of 12 Group! Clearly the Minister knew not the difference between a Spitfire or Hurricane, much less the disposition of Fighter Command's Groups. We were not impressed.

On September 20th, Pilot Officer Jones was posted from 64 to 19 Squadron at Fowlmere (in 12 Group!). By that time, as we have read before, 19 Squadron was operating as a top cover Spitfire squadron in Douglas Bader's so-called 'Big Wing'. Richard therefore enjoys an enviable perspective on the tactical argument of the day, having flown Spitfires during the Battle of Britain in both 11 and 12 Groups.

On October 28th, a single Gruppe of Ju 88s headed for London, protected by three *Jagdgeschwadern* of Me 109s. Soon 19 Squadron was up, Pilot Officer Jones flying Spitfire P7432:-

> When patrolling over the Tenterden area at 29,000 feet, the Controller informed us that as there were apparently no enemy aircraft in the vicinity we could 'pancake'. I was 'Arse-end Charlie' and relaxed slightly as we descended to 20,000 feet. Suddenly about four feet of my starboard wing just peeled off. My initial thought that it was a poor show on a new aircraft. Then a loud bang followed and a hole appeared above the undercarriage. I was obviously the target of an enemy fighter positioned up sun. Immediately I took evasive action but simultaneously my engine cut out, so suddenly I was in a high speed stall and spin. As my radio was U/S I was unable to inform the Squadron, the other pilots of which returned to base blissfully unaware that I had been shot down.
>
> As the aircraft's controls were not responding I did not recover from the spin until at 10,000 feet, and at that time I realised that the hood was jammed shut. Subsequently I crash-landed with a dead engine in one of only two suitable fields in a heavily wooded area just outside Hawkhurst. Unfortunately I did so amongst a flock of sheep and unfortunately several were killed. I was rescued by the Army and taken first to the Hawkhurst doctor who treated a flesh wound to my leg, then to their Mess prior to returning safely to Fowlmere.
>
> My Spitfire had a broken propeller and radiator, a few holes and some missing parts but was otherwise relatively undamaged. For some reason the incident was not recorded in the 19 Squadron Operations Record Book, but in my logbook I wrote 'Shot down and crash-landed at Hawkhurst, Kent. Killed three sheep. What a bloody mess!!!', which it was.

On November 15th, Richard was returned to 64 Squadron, with which he remained until April 1941, when seconded to the Ministry of Aircraft Production and 'lent' to the De Havilland company as a test pilot. Consequently Richard test flew Spitfires and Hurricanes that had been repaired at the factory, a job which he retained until leaving the RAF (as a Flight Lieutenant) in 1946.

Now retired from a post war career in the motor industry and a long spell as a part-time court usher, Richard is still enjoying life and retirement, aged 80. Together with his truly charming wife Elizabeth and daughter Susan, Richard Jones has been another welcome guest and friend at our events. Dubbed the 'Peter Pan of the Battle of Britain' by all at Ramrod, given that he never seems to age, Richard has the ability to communicate with all, including youngsters. It gave me great pleasure, therefore, to take Richard (and Bob Morris, of whom more later) to my old school at Sibford Ferris in the Cotswolds in November 2000. There we gave a presentation to pupils regarding the Battle of Britain, the experience being greatly enjoyed and appreciated by all involved.

Richard Jones pictured at home by the author in 1991.

Chapter Nine

Sergeant Reg Nutter

Once more we find that Reginald Charles Nutter was a VR pilot, having joined in March 1939. Reg received his flying badge in April 1940:-

Just as French resistance was collapsing, Sergeant Don Hulbert and myself were posted to 601, a Hurricane squadron at Tangmere. The unit had been knocked about in France, where it had spent some time prior to our departure. We were soon posted to 257 Squadron at Hendon, which was a newly formed squadron working up on Spitfires.

At Hendon we went through the usual reporting in procedure and met our new CO, Squadron Leader Bayne. I was assigned to 'A' Flight, which was commanded by Flight Lieutenant Hugh Beresford. Our Spitfires were arriving in twos and threes, and after a 10-minute flight check in a Miles Master with Beresford, I was authorised to make my first Spitfire flight.

The weather was very warm and I was warned by the groundcrew not to spend too long taxiing around or the aircraft would overheat. On take off I was very impressed by the power of the Merlin engine and the Spitfire's rapid climb. In the air I found it a beautiful aircraft to handle because it was so light on the controls. I was somewhat disconcerted when it became time to land, as Hendon looked like a small green postage stamp, completely surrounded by houses. However, I managed to make a very credible landing and, feeling quite proud of myself, took off and made another one.

Most of the pilots joining the Squadron had neither before been on a fighter squadron or flown Spitfires. As a result the next three weeks were spent familiarising ourselves with the Spitfire. In the first week of June, we learned that we would be re-equipped with Hawker Hurricanes and shortly afterwards this type of aircraft began arriving at Hendon. On June 14th, I made my first trip in a Hurricane and found it much heavier at the controls, far less responsive and somewhat slower than the Spitfire.

During the working up period, Don Hulbert and myself were sent to RAF Uxbridge for a radio procedure course. This proved to be quite interesting as it had a two-fold purpose – to train pilots in R/T procedures and to train the Fighter Controllers who would later control us from Operations Rooms. Marked out on the playing fields was a large map of the British Isles and a part of Western Europe. We pilots were given tricycles, which had formerly been used to sell ice cream! In the box at the front was a TR9 radio, which, at the time, was standard aircraft equipment. We wore headphones and were surrounded by a set of blinker like boards, which restricted our vision. The driving chain and sprockets were arranged in such a way that when we pedalled 25 times the wheel moved round just once! Thus our speed across the maps matched the speed of fighter aircraft across the ground at normal throttle settings. Down in the stadium a complete Operations Room had been built. This was fully manned by trainee Controllers, WAAF Plotters etc. On top of the stadium was a spotter who passed our position, and the position of the person designated as the 'enemy', down to the Operations Room. The 'Controllers' could then vector us by radio to make interceptions. We both learned a lot from the course but found it somewhat difficult to sit down on our final return to the Squadron. Pedalling around in the hot sun in a serge uniform made one quite sore in a certain part of one's anatomy!

By the end of June, Squadron Leader Bayne had us all whipped into pretty good shape. We had done a good deal of formation flying, air-to-ground and air-to-air firing. Around the beginning of July, the Squadron moved to Northolt where we practised 'scrambling' from real dispersal points. The airfield was also big enough for us to practise dusk and night landings.

From my logbook it appears that the Squadron was declared fully operational on July 20th, 1940. At about this time a change of command occurred with Squadron Leader Harkness replacing Bayne. We spent a good deal of the rest of the month operating out of Hawkinge, near Folkestone, with a return to Northolt each evening.

Early in August three of our pilots, Pilot Officer the Hon. David Coke, Pilot Officer Carl Capon and myself, were chosen to perform VIP escort duties. My log shows a flight to Christchurch escorting an American VIP, and on August 7th & 8th we escorted the Prime Minister, Winston Churchill, who was a passenger in a De Havilland Flamingo piloted by Flight Lieutenant Blenner-Hassett. The route was Hendon to Northcoates, Manby, Coltishall to Hendon. This trip remains vivid in my memory as the PM persuaded his pilot to do some very low flying, for his personal amusement, across the Wash!

Pilot Officer The Hon David Coke

During the first half of August, the Squadron also operated on a daily basis out of North Weald to provide escort to convoys proceeding up or down the East Coast. We also operated out of Tangmere on a daily basis to provide similar cover to shipping in the English Channel. On August 8th, whilst on a convoy patrol, the Squadron tried to intercept some bombers which were attacking a convoy, but we were jumped by enemy fighters. In this first major engagement we lost three pilots: Flight Lieutenant Hall, Flying Officer D'Arcy Irvine and Sergeant Smith. This loss, coupled with the recent and unpopular change of command, caused a sharp drop in morale.

On August 15th we moved to Debden. This airfield had only just been completed and was very modern. From here we operated out of Martlesham Heath on a daily basis. Again we carried out many convoy patrols but also intercepted some of the larger raids in the London area. Towards the end of the month, Debden was heavily bombed and put more or less out of action. We had to move to Martlesham until things were sorted. It was during this period that Pilot Officers Chomley and Maffett were killed.

September was a very busy month with the Squadron flying many sorties and getting involved in plenty of fighting. During this phase the Germans were putting up really large fleets of bombers with heavy fighter escorts. We suffered further casualties, including Flight Lieutenant Beresford, Flying Officer Mitchell and Pilot Officer Bonseigneur.

Hugh Beresford was replaced as commander of 'A' Flight by Flight Lieutenant Peter Brothers, who came to us from 32 Squadron. At this time Harkness was also replaced as Commanding Officer by Squadron Leader Robert Stanford Tuck. This turned out to be very good news. We found Tuck to be a charismatic leader and this, combined with his exceptional combat record, gave me great confidence. His style of leadership contrasted greatly with that of his predecessor. Squadron Leader Tuck would make suggestions to the Controller as to how we might be better placed to make an interception, whereas Harkness would merely follow all instructions without question. When Tuck took us over morale was low. Under his inspired leadership there was a tremendous improvement. In many ways Tuck was an individualist but he could also play as part of the team. He would always go out of his way to provide other pilots with sound advice.

On September 2nd, we were patrolling off North Foreland when I managed to get some good bursts at a 109 which had swung in front of me whilst attempting to attack the Squadron from the rear. He immediately dived, streaming coolant, but I lost sight of him in the thick haze. On September 3rd, whilst intercepting a force of bombers attacking North Weald, I stupidly allowed myself to watch the fall of bombs across the aerodrome, instead of watching my tail. I was promptly pounced upon by an Me 110. Although my Hurricane got quite badly shot up and leaked petrol all over me, and despite having received shrapnel wounds o my right side, I managed to make it safely back to Martlesham Heath.

On October 7th we moved to North Weald. The daylight raids by large bomber fleets had ceased by this time, but the night raids on London and other cities had already begun. During daylight the Germans began employing Me 109s and 110s as fighter-bombers. These were nuisance raids intended to keep the British defences at a constant state of alert and demoralise the civilian population by the constant sounding of air raid warning sirens. These sorties tended to be flown at very high altitudes and formations were mixed with fighters not carrying bombs. Intercepting them was tiring work because of the high altitude involved, as in those days we had no pressurised cabin or flying suit.

For me personally the Battle of Britain remains a vivid kaleidoscope of memories. I recall trying to warn Pilot Officer Capon that he was about to be attacked by an Me 109 but my radio was U/S. I remember The Hon David Coke returning from a battle over Portsmouth during which a German bullet had nicked him in the little finger of his throttle hand. Once I chased a lone Do 17 reconnaissance bomber in and out of the clouds along the South Coast whilst listening to American jazz music that was coming over our Squadron's frequency. Vivid memories all.

One incident not mentioned by Reg is the stirring low-level raid on North Weald by II/LG 2's Me 109 fighter-bombers, escorted by Major Adolf Galland's JG 26. This perfectly executed surprise attack left 19 RAF personnel dead and 42 more wounded. Flight Lieutenant Peter Brothers:-

We all dived under a table when the attack came in! My car, an open 3-litre Bentley, was parked outside and I was livid to discover that a near-miss bomb had filled it with soil, which took forever to clean out!

A dozen 109s hit the airfield from two sides, causing mayhem. Some Hurricanes were trying to get up, but as the warning had come so late, it was hopeless. A bomb exploded beneath Sergeant Girdwood's Hurricane, shortly after becoming unstuck. The aircraft crashed in flames just beyond the aerodrome's Northwest perimeter, killing the pilot. Flight Lieutenant 'Cowboy' Blatchford managed to take off, as did Sergeant Nutter and the Polish Pilot Officer Franek Surma. A skirmish rapidly developed above the smoking airfield. Blatchford thrusted at a 109, but was himself hit hard in a head-on attack by *Hauptmann* Gerhard Schöpfel, *Gruppenkommandeur* of III/JG 26. Fortunately Blatchford managed to crash-land his damaged fighter back at base. Reg Nutter was also in the fight, and attacked Schöpfel from the beam, but without result.

Flight Lieutenant 'C o w b o y' Blatchford

Pilot Officer Surma had seen the bombs falling, as he was taxying across the aerodrome and preparing to take off. A bomb exploded on his left-hand side, shaking his aircraft forcibly, although he managed to get safely airborne through the lethal shot and shell directed at him. Climbing rapidly to 3,000 feet, the gallant Pole was also attacked by Schöpfel. A cannon shell exploded in the Hurricane's cockpit and this was soon filled with white smoke. Out of control, the Hurricane plunged into a spiral dive. After a struggle, Surma safely baled out at 1,000 feet. According to the Squadron Intelligence Report, he made 'a successful parachute descent, landing in a treetop near Matching. After quickly convincing a Home Guard that he was a Pole and not a German, he was given two complimentary whiskies and driven back to the aerodrome. He had lost both flying boots when jumping out of the plane, received a black eye but was otherwise unharmed'.

The Germans, however, did not escape unscathed. Three of the North Weald raiders were brought down. One enemy pilot was killed when his aircraft crashed at Goldhanger in Essex, another was captured and the third baled out but died refusing medical help from his British captors.

It was the story of Franek Surma, in fact, that brought Reg Nutter and I into contact nearly 20 years ago. As some readers may know, the story of Flying Officer Surma was the subject of my second book, *The Invisible Thread: A Spitfire's Tale* (Ramrod, 1992). My interest was stimulated by the fact that Surma baled out of a 308 Squadron Spitfire, R6644, which consequently crashed near my home on May 11th, 1941 (albeit 20 years before I was born). Having traced local eyewitnesses and starting to research the incident, as a complete amateur, I was moved to discover that the 25-year old Surma had been shot down over the Channel on November 8th, 1941, and remained 'Missing in Action'. Going on to trace numerous pilots who had not only flown R6644 but also with Surma himself, I was able to reconstruct the period, and in particular the air battle in which this decorated Polish fighter ace lost his life.

In 1987, the Malvern Spitfire Team excavated the crash site of R6644 at a public event organised to raise money for the RAFA's 'Wings Appeal'. Our guests of honour were Polish Battle of Britain veterans

Pilot Officer Franek Surma pictured before the war, in Polish Air Force uniform, at his niece's christening at Galkowice, Poland.

Squadron Leaders 'Gandy' Drobinski DFC and Ludwik Martel, both of whom unveiled the cairn that we had built in nearby Jennet Tree Lane, Madresfield, to Franek Surma's memory. Ultimately we were able to trace Franek Surma's two surviving sisters in Poland, who were both astonished and extremely moved to learn of our efforts to ensure that their brother's memory would live on. In 1988, I received an equally moving letter from them, part of which I reproduce below:-

> Through your letter you have aroused our memories and have shown how wonderful people can be. Many special thanks go to you and we will be praying for your success in life, prayers for a person who is now very dear to us. May God take care of you and the organisation that you have created. We are so happy that there is still someone to light a candle for Franek on All Souls' Day. We are also happy because the memorial erected to him serves as his grave, a symbol that he can see from heaven. We have always been worried because Franek has no known grave. Now we are all at peace, thanks to you and your friends.

Having been involved with Battle of Britain research for so long, I am acutely aware that, as with any other activity, there are highs and lows.

The Surma letter remains an extreme high.

A piston and liner from the Merlin engine of Spitfire R6644, safely abandoned by Pilot Officer Surma in 1941 and recovered by the author and friends in 1987.

In 1988, our exhibition of the Surma and R6644 story opened at a museum in Worcester, and attendance figures surpassed our wildest expectations. As a result of this interest, when the time came to dismantle the show it was made into a travelling show which later toured the country and was enjoyed by countless people.

By 1992, in my professional life I was a Local Beat Officer concerned with the problems caused by local youngsters. In an effort to divert them from petty crime and anti-social behaviour we founded the 'Surma Memorial Trust for Youth'. The object of this formally registered charity was to uphold Franek Surma's story as an example to young people, and in his name provide financial assistance to projects working to improve the quality of life for local youngsters. When *The Invisible Thread* was published, local businesses were persuaded to sponsor production of a fine art print of the book's superb jacket painting, this having been specially produced by award wining aviation artist Mark Postlethwaite G.Av.A. In a refreshing example of the young and old working together for the common good, veterans kindly signed the prints, the book, prints, Trust and Ramrod Publications all being launched concurrently at a high profile event, attended by nearly 40 former wartime fighter pilots, held at Great Malvern. Ultimately, some £15,000 was raised for and distributed accordingly by the Trust which, due to me being posted elsewhere, was wound up in December 1997. At that time, the Trust's outstanding balance was presented to Malvern Youth Centre and financed the purchase of vital computer equipment. At the official winding up, a plaque telling the Surma story was unveiled at the Youth Centre by Mrs Barbara Sykes, the niece of a Polish Battle of Britain pilot, Flying Officer Franek Gruszka, who was killed in action on August 18th, 1940.

Having started the Franek Surma ball rolling, as it were, back in 1986, things do seem to keep happening which inexorably draw me back to it. A couple of years ago, for example, I received a surprise visit at home from a cousin of Franek Surma's, who lived in the UK and happened to be in the area. With him he brought a snapshot of Franek in his Polish Air Force uniform, taken shortly before the war at his niece's Christening. More recently I have received an email inviting me to Poland for the opening of a school in Galkowice, Surma's hometown near the Czech border, which has been named after their local hero. Unfortunately family commitments prevented my attendance, but it is tremendous to know that our project caused such widespread interest and recognition for this previously all but forgotten hero.

The Malvern Spitfire Team's memorial cairn dedicated to Flying Officer Surma (as he later became) in Jennet Tree Lane, Madresfield, Worcestershire. The wreaths, left to right, are from the Team, the Polish Air Force Association and the Great Malvern Branch of the RAFA.

Chapter Ten

Flight Lieutenant Peter Brothers DFC

Peter Malam Brothers was another early correspondent who became a friend. Born at Westerham in Kent on September 30th, 1917, being a young man of means he learnt to fly privately at the age of 16. Commissioned into the RAF in 1936, later that year he received his flying brevet and joined 32 Squadron at Biggin Hill. By late 1938 he was a Flight Commander, a position Peter still occupied when war broke out. In May 1940, 32 Squadron fought in France, and Flight Lieutenant Brothers opened his account as a fighter pilot when he destroyed an Me 109 on May 19th.

Having survived the Battle of France and the opening shots of the Battle of Britain, Peter was transferred to command a flight in 257 Squadron at Debden on September 9th. There he served under Squadron Leader Bob Stanford Tuck, and continued his success against the enemy. On September 13th, he was awarded the DFC (a Bar followed in 1943, and a DSO in 1944).

After the Battle of Britain, Peter formed and commanded an Australian Spitfire squadron, 457, and later led the Wings at Tangmere, Exeter, Culmhead and Milfield. After the war, he left the RAF and joined the colonial service in Kenya for a couple of years prior to coming home and re-joining the air force. Following a number of important

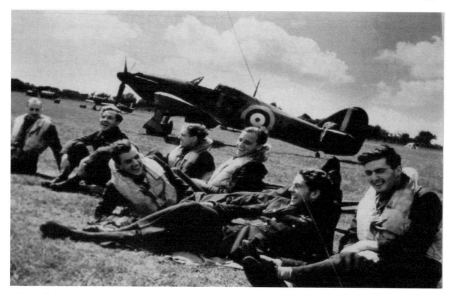

One of the most famous Battle of Britain photographs ever taken: 32 Squadron await the call to scramble at Hawkinge, August 1940. Peter Brothers is at centre.

appointments and commands, and having been made a CBE, Peter retired as an Air Commodore.

At the time of writing, Peter Brothers is a most active Deputy Chairman of the Battle of Britain Fighter Association, in which capacity we were proud that he kindly wrote the Foreword to my *Battle of Britain: The Photographic Kaleidoscope Volume III*, produced to mark the 60th anniversary. We were also honoured to welcome both the Chairman, Air Chief Marshal Sir Christopher Foxley-Norris (who wrote the Foreword to *Volume IV*) and Air Commodore Brothers at the launch of my *Volume II* and Robert Rudhall's memorable *Battle of Britain: The Movie*.

Another enduring personal memory is the evening spent at RAF Bentley Priory in September 1997, as the Battle of Britain Fighter Association's guest at the annual reunion dinner. Every year a Memorial Flight Spitfire from Coningsby provides a nostalgic display for these distinguished airmen. At the appointed time, we all went outside and awaited the Spitfire's arrival with growing anticipation. Throughout the wait I stood chatting to Peter, until our conversation was lost in the roar of a Merlin! As ever, Squadron Leader Paul Day provided an excellent display, which brought smiles and applause all round.

In selecting an extract from our protracted correspondence, ultimately I decided that the best thing would be to reproduce the Foreword that Peter so kindly contributed, and which I enjoyed reading immensely.

> This third *Battle of Britain: The Photographic Kaleidoscope*, written by Dilip Sarkar and produced by his wife Anita, is a remarkable tribute to the diligent research that we have come to expect from this author. Whilst security restrictions, coupled with the difficulties of obtaining film in 1940 meant that opportunities to record the period on film were limited, Dilip has unearthed a truly amazing collection of personal photographs, many of which have not been published before. Naturally the book brought back many memories for me, and was thought provoking.
>
> It was inevitable, of course, that not all of the pilots who fought in the Battle of Britain achieved the mystic figure of five enemy aircraft shot down, thereby confirming 'ace status. Indeed, these were the majority who played a valiant part and without whom the Battle of Britain could not have been won. The pictures of them in this book pay an eloquent tribute to their efforts.

Another in the same sequence, Peter Brothers again at centre.

Generally speaking, these were the gallant youngsters who joined the RAF VR pre-war. When called up, by having already learned to fly, they were ready to convert to and gain some experience of the Hurricane or Spitfire, the aircraft that they were to operate in battle. Or they were the ones who joined in the outbreak of war and were rushed through flying training, followed by considerably less experience of the aircraft they were to fly in combat.

The remaining non-regular element were the members of the then Auxiliary Air Force, later becoming the 'Royal', the so-called 'weekend flyers' who had the advantage in most cases of already being equipped with Hurricanes and Spitfires, or other operational types.

Reflecting after the war on our losses during the Battle of Britain, I noted that in my squadron, No 32 at Biggin Hill, of our pre-war pilots there were some who had been shot down and baled out unhurt, or burnt, or wounded, or both, but none were killed. Our losses were the 'new boys' who never had the time or opportunity not only to learn or be taught the tricks of the trade, but also to know the performance advantages and limits of their aircraft and how to exploit them. Tragically, they paid the ultimate penalty for their inexperience.

An example springs to mind. Prior to the Battle of Britain, operating over France as a flight commander, I naturally took our latest 'new boy' under my wing to fly as my Number Two. Suddenly I had that feeling we all experience at some time that I was being watched. Glancing in my rear-view mirror I was startled to see, immediately behind me and between my Number Two and me, the biggest and fattest Me 109 – ever! As I instantly took evasive action his front end lit up as he fired. I escaped unscathed, he climbed and vanished as I was doing a tight turn, looking for my Number Two. There he was, good man, cutting the corner to get back into position, as I thought, until he opened fire –at me! Suggesting on the radio that his action was unpopular, as there were no other aircraft in sight we wended our way home. Not only had he not warned me of the 109's presence or fired at it, he had had an easy shot at me but missed! I dealt a blow to his jauntiness by removing him from operations for two days intensive gunnery training. Sadly it failed to help him survive.

As so much time has now elapsed since this country's last major war, and the key to victory provided by the Battle of Britain, I am constantly being surprised by the interest shown in it by people from all walks of life and from so many different countries throughout the world. The interest of historians and military men I can understand, but they are the few, not the many, whose demands for information seems insatiable. Fortunately there are books like this to provide not merely information but also fascinating reading.

Air Commodore Peter Malan Brothers CBE DSO DFC, and Deputy Chairman of the Battle of Britain Fighter Association, at a Ramrod book launch in 2000.

Chapter Eleven

Corporal Bob Morris

Bob Morris was, in fact, the first person that I ever had the privilege to meet who was actually personally involved in the Battle of Britain. Of course I had read numerous books and seen a host of television programmes and films, but there was a very definite thrill attached to meeting someone who was 'there', and indeed hearing of their first-hand experiences. The location for our meeting was an unlikely venue (and I can see Bob sat there smiling as he reads this): Bob's potting shed! This was no ordinary garden shed, however, as within Bob had created a den in which he could recall those golden years. We were soon engrossed in conversation, as Bob enthusiastically remembered 1940. Enthusiasm is a part of Bob's great natural charm, in fact, as he remains just as enthusiastic now for his beloved Spitfires, and in that has always been an inspiration to me personally.

Hailing from rural Herefordshire, Bob, just 19-years old in 1940, remembers those far off days:-

I joined the RAF before the war started, and being more interested in the technical rather than the flying side I studied aeronautical engineering at RAF Halton. I was still on my course when war came, but things like sport etc were reduced to move us on quickly. In May 1940, therefore, I passed out of Halton as an Airman 1st Class and discovered that I had been posted to 66 Squadron in Coltishall.

My first glimpse of a Spitfire was from the bus that travelled alongside the airfield for a short distance – what a thrill, every young man's dream!

We shared the airfield with the Hurricanes of 242 Squadron, but we were not there long as we moved to Kenley, in 11 Group, right down in the thick of it. We arrived there on September 3rd, 1940, it was an absolute shambles, there was hardly a building left standing. As we drove around the aerodrome to our assembly point, I saw a car park full of vehicles; there was not one undamaged by bullets or shrapnel. There were shelters destroyed, buildings flattened. We were only there for a week but that short time was absolutely devastating. During that week I think we lost eight pilots, so by the end of it we were practically out of action.

From a ground viewpoint we had to learn very quickly about air raids which were incoming thick and fast. Once I looked up and saw five parachutes descending. We were dispersed around the edge of the airfield with plenty of space between each Spitfire. We could not put them either in a group or inside a hangar for fear of them being destroyed together. It meant that we had to work on them in the open, often without any cover when a raid occurred. They had built some blast pens at Kenley, but no-where near enough, so you could be a quarter of a mile away from the shelter. It is perhaps surprising but you do get used to it. We used to carry on working after the siren had gone, right up until the Germans were practically overhead. If you then left your aircraft and lay down on the ground some distance away from it, the chances of being killed by a bomb were remote. Strafing was a bit more hazardous, but the greatest danger was bomb-blast, i.e. what it actually threw up into the air. If a bomb exploded near a road, building or runway then huge slabs and chunks of concrete and masonry could come falling down on you.

On September 10th, 66 Squadron moved to Gravesend, which was just a civilian flying club's airfield. We were the only squadron there, at what was Biggin Hill's satellite field. We looked down on the River Thames, opposite Tilbury Docks, and I remember seeing bombs hitting large floating oil tanks there. Fortunately we were not bombed there, we would have been hard to put out of action anyway as there was just one hangar, a dining room and small hut for flying control.

Bob Morris, right, identifies artefacts from Spitfire R6644 with Polish Battle of Britain pilots Squadron Leaders Gandy Drobinski DFC and Ludwik Martel VM KW, September 1987.

The model Spitfire presented by Ramrod Publications to Bob Morris, made by Andrew Long and featuring items from a 66 Squadron Spitfire that Bob actually worked on in 1940! (*Andrew Long*)

Life was exhausting. At Gravesend we had half a day off every 10 days, which we used to spend fast asleep! We were working from dawn to dusk. We lived at first in a restaurant called 'Laughing Waters', but were then moved to Cobham Hall. Off-duty, the officers frequented their favoured restaurant, we 'ORs' used the local pub and never the twain shall meet.

We were still in action flying from Gravesend, and lost more pilots. One of them, an American called Pilot Officer Reilley, I had got to know quite well. One afternoon I was asleep on my half-day when the Sergeant bellowed that he wanted us all out in best blue. We got dressed, boarded transport and ended up providing the Guard of Honour at poor old Reilley's funeral. On the way back, someone mentioned that Reilley's wife had recently given birth to a baby boy. Little did I know then that I would meet that 'baby boy', John Reilley, at 66 Squadron's first reunion in 1983!

We spent September 15th, later celebrated as 'Battle of Britain Day', at Gravesend. We watched the German aircraft coming, heading for

London, or the vapour trails in the sky. We were always relieved when they passed overhead and carried on! That September, as we were close to the river, there would often be ground mist that could last all day. It could be such thick fog that no aircraft could take off, but at least they could not bomb us either. On such days our work would be complete by mid-afternoon, at which time a football would appear. We never picked a side, just joined in with whichever side appeared to be winning! On one occasion we could hear German aircraft circling round in the fog above, looking for us. Suddenly they dropped a parachute flare but someone put it out and we carried on playing! The Germans then flew off. No one had run for shelter, that was how accustomed to it all we had become.

It was towards the end of our time at Gravesend that we began to see the DFCs and DFMs awarded to our pilots. Of course I will always remember the sight of aircraft damaged in combat. One day Pilot Officer 'Bogle' Bodie returned with his port mainplane badly knocked about by a cannon shell, I had to rip part of the aileron off which he took as a souvenir. One Spitfire came in making an awful whistling noise caused by a single bullet hole right through a propeller blade! As we had no spare blades we had to smooth out the hole before drilling corresponding holes in the other two blades. It then flew for another fortnight in that unusual condition!

On October 30th, we moved to West Malling. A squadron move is a complicated business and I could never understand why we were put to so much trouble for so short a distance. Someone said it was to confuse the enemy – it certainly confused us! A week later we were moved to Biggin Hill, and we found that station a shambles too. There were very few buildings left standing and there were no billets. We ended up commandeering a Women's Institute building where we slept on straw. So far as the airfield was concerned, because of the damaged installations it was back to working out in the open. Another round of scrambles, sirens, work and inspection procedures, just a hard and very unromantic slog.

Again, we used to watch the Germans going over, mainly fighters by this time, and we even saw some dogfights from Biggin Hill. I saw one German bomber shot down and four parachutes appeared, two of them on fire. We saw these unfortunate Germans fall faster and faster until the parachute had completely burnt away and they fell to their deaths. Although enemy aircraft were being shot down we rarely saw one as this was dealt with by Maintenance Units. At Biggin Hill, however, I had the opportunity to look over an Me 109 which was on the station and virtually complete. I looked in the cockpit and in my opinion the instrumentation was nowhere up to a Spitfire's standard, very poor.

On February 24th, 1941, we moved from Biggin Hill to Exeter, in 10 Group. There we joined 504 Squadron's Hurricanes and together our fighters provided some protection to the docks at Bristol and Plymouth. One moonlit night we went outside to watch the German bombers going over but they dropped incendiaries on the airfield. It was a successful raid as these damn things blazed away every where. It was chaos. People were running hither and thither with fire extinguishers, there was a Wellington bomber blazing away, .303 ammunition was popping off in all directions, Spitfires were blown up and huts were wrecked. Strangely, 504 Squadron escaped unscathed every time we were attacked!

One morning our pilots were supposed to be on stand-by but, for a variety of reasons, were not at dispersal on the appointed hour. As a punishment we were sent to Perranporth, in Cornwall, and it was there that my time with 66 Squadron came to an end and I was posted overseas.

So that is the story of my time with a Battle of Britain Spitfire squadron. Looking back on it we were so young, 60 years later I look back and think that I would be much more frightened if I had to do it all again. Being young we took the whole thing very lightly. I now reflect upon those days with great pride and affection, and it has given me enormous pleasure over the years to be closely involved with Dilip Sarkar and his many projects, firstly with the Malvern Spitfire Team and more recently by supporting his efforts via Ramrod Publications. I am also a member of the Battle of Britain Society and I am delighted that the Battle of Britain no longer looks like being consigned to the dustbin of British history. People should know what was at stake that summer, and what they will always owe, therefore, those of my generation who were there and able to do their bit.

Bob has never missed any of our events, and as a token of our appreciation we recently presented him with a model 66 Squadron Spitfire made by Andrew Long. Mounted on the base were some items from Pilot Officer Reilley's 66 Squadron Spitfire, on which Bob worked during the Battle of Britain, and the funeral of which pilot he attended. Not surprisingly this nostalgic and tangible piece of Bob's Battle of Britain past now occupies pride of place in the Morris household.

Bob Morris pictured at a recent Ramrod book signing

(Andrew Long)

Chapter Twelve

Pilot Officer Harry Welford

During the course of my research into the service of Franek Surma, it was interesting to talk to a number of pilots who had flown with him on the several squadrons with which he saw action during the Battle of Britain (151, 607 & 257). Amongst them was Harry Welford, who, in direct contrast to the majority of other pilots featured in this book, was a pre-war auxiliary member of 607 'County of Durham' Squadron. We have already touched upon what the Auxiliary Air Force was, but the following account, from (the sadly late) Air Vice-Marshal Johnnie Johnson indicates the importance of social standing to the auxiliaries:-

I went along for this interview with the senior officer there (in 1938, with a view to joining the Auxiliary Air Force), who, knowing that I came from Leicestershire said "With whom do you hunt, Johnson?"
I said "Hunt, Sir?"
He said "Yes, Johnson, hunt. With whom do you hunt?"
I said "Well I don't hunt, Sir, I shoot."
He said "Oh! Well thank you then, Johnson, that will be all!"

Clearly the fact that I could shoot game on the wing impressed him not one bit. Had I been socially acceptable, however, by hunting with lord-so-and-so, things would have been different, but back then that is what the auxiliaries were like, and do not forget that many members were of independent means, which I certainly wasn't!

Johnnie, who went on to become the RAF's top scoring fighter pilot of WW2, still keen to do his bit, instead joined firstly the Leicestershire Yoemanry, a Territorial Army unit, and then the RAFVR. The rest, as they say, is history (but see *Johnnie Johnson: Spitfire Top Gun, Part One*, Ramrod, 2002).

Harry Welford, however, describes how he came to be an auxiliary airman:-

During 1939, my cousin Robert got permission to take me up to the Auxiliary Air Force base at Usworth and give me a 'flip', parlance for 'flying experience'. It was a fine day and ideal to get the feeling of 'no longer being earthbound', as my cousin put it. However, I knew that what goes up must come down again, so I was nervous. I was strapped in the front cockpit of an Avro dual control trainer with Robert in the rear. This seemed odd to me as I had expected the passenger to sit behind. Anyway we taxied out and Robert spoke to me through the intercom, swung into wind and took off. After a circuit of the airfield we did a trip over the local countryside pointing out such landmarks as Penshaw Monument, the River Wear, and, of course, Sunderland and Newcastle further north. All of these sights will remain in my memory as pointers to the aerodrome itself. My cousin asked how I liked it and my response was enthusiastic, whereupon he suggested performing the odd aerobatic. Before I could respond he dived steeply and performed a loop followed by a slow roll. My stomach was not feeling so good and I was quietly sick over the side. Robert must have seen my distress because he went down to land, by which time I was all right again. We joked about it but one of the senior officers must have spotted the mess in the cockpit and gave poor Robert a ticking off for doing aerobatics during an air experience exercise. He then made Robert clean up the cockpit.

Robert's aerobatics did not put Harry off, however, for on his 22nd birthday, December 4th, 1938, he was accepted for training with 607 'County of Durham' Squadron. In a way, the Auxiliary Air Force sounds a bit like Boy Scouts with aeroplanes, as Harry continues:-

The Squadron's annual summer camp in 1939 was actually a prelude to war. None of us would be out of uniform for the next six years. Many would not survive for one year, let alone six. The summer camp concerned was at Abbotsinch, near Glasgow, which was the home base of 602 Squadron, another Auxiliary unit which was holding summer camp elsewhere. We pilots flew our machines up there whilst the ground crews were transported by road in advance of our arrival, erecting tents and marquees for servicing and messing facilities. The Gladiators took off in squadron formation and were a sight to be proud of, whilst we trainees followed in our Avro Tutors, in open order, led by the instructors. I was very proud to be flying solo on the longest cross-country I had done, although I was following the leading instructors and just wished that some of my fancied girlfriends could see me now!

In May 1939, I was commissioned into the Auxiliary Air Force as a Pilot Officer, and called to full-time service on August 24th. In October I completed my Service Flying Training and then went to 6 OTU at Sutton Bridge to learn how to fly Hurricanes. There we became familiar with all aspects of our Hurricanes and concentrated on aerobatics and more unconventional versions of them to avoid enemy attacks. We also did a lot of formation and simulated attacks and fighter tactics. A favourite exercise was to go up in pairs with an experienced pilot and then he would tell you over the R/T to follow him in all the manoeuvres he carried out. He aimed to lose you, and generally did, then got on your tail and the situation was reversed. Afterwards you discussed the different tactics of defence and attack, and the instructor would then advise you according to his experience.

Harry continues, describing his first encounter with the Hawker Hurricane:-

Having previously only flown biplanes with fixed-pitch airscrews and no flaps, I required instruction on these additional facilities. I was therefore given dual instruction in a Harvard aircraft, which had most of the Hurricane's refinements, but not all, and no where near the power of its 1,280-HP Rolls-Royce Merlin engine. It was in the air when I started worrying how, in the name of heaven, I was going to get this thing called a Hurricane down again. I did a few manoeuvres and a couple of circuits, got my wheels and flaps down, my God how the speed dropped and how the attitude changed! I was coming down too steeply, I opened the throttle and she assumed a more gentle engine-assisted approach. I touched down and throttled back but then realised that I had not got much more aerodrome to pull up in. Hell, I was on the ground and intended to stay there. It being a grass airfield, I did not roll too far but far enough even with judicious braking to be just short of chopping the far hedge with my propeller. Nobody worried very much because I was sent off formation flying for the very next trip the same day.

At 1230 hours on August 15th, we were going off duty for 24 hours leave when the whole squadron was called to Readiness. We heard from the Group Operations Room that there was a big 'flap' on, that is a warning of imminent enemy action along the NE coast. We waited out at dispersal points, at 'Flights', for half an hour, then scrambled in squadron formation. I was in a feverish state of excitement and quickly took off and climbed up to our operational height of 20,000' ready to patrol the coast. We kept receiving messages over the R/T of 40 or 50 plus 'Bogeys' approaching Newcastle from the north. Although we patrolled for over half an hour, we never saw a thing. Just as I was expecting the order to 'Pancake', I heard the senior flight commander shout 'Tally Ho!', and 'Tally Ho' it was! There, on our port side at 9,000' must have been 120 bombers, all with swastikas and German crosses as large as life, having the gross impertinence to cruise down Northumberland and Durham's NE coast. These were the people who were going to bomb Newcastle and Sunderland where our families and friends lived, 607 Squadron being an Auxiliary unit raised from the local area.

I'd never seen anything like it. They were in two groups, one of about 70 and the other about 40, like two swarms of bees. There was no time to wait and we took up position and delivered No 3 attacks in sections. As only three machines at a time, in formation, attacked a line of 20 bombers, I just couldn't see how their gunners could miss us. We executed our attack, however, and despite the fact that I thought it was me being hit all over the place, it was their machines that started dropping out of the sky. In my excitement, during the next attack I only narrowly missed one of our own machines whilst doing a 'split arse' breakaway - there couldn't have been more than two feet between us! Eventually, spotting most of the enemy aircraft dropping down with only their undercarriages damaged, I chased a Heinkel and filled that poor devil with lead until first one, then the other engine stopped. I then enjoyed the sadistic satisfaction of watching the bomber crash into the sea. With the one I reckoned to have damaged during our first attack, these were my first bloods, and so I was naturally elated. The squadron suffered no losses, but claimed six He 111s and two Do 17s destroyed, five He 111s and one Do 17 probably destroyed, and four He 111s and one Do 17 damaged, although we now know that in fact, there were no Do 17s amongst the German formation.

I shall always remember September 8th, 1940, because this was the day after the evening that Betty Elise and I became engaged, but our move to Tangmere, in 11 Group, was confirmed that day. We were to relieve 43 Squadron who CO, 'Tubby' Badger, had been shot down earlier in September and since which time the Squadron had been led by Flight Lieutenant Tom Morgan. Now, barely half the original complement of pilots were capable of operational duties.

Of course it was a tragedy so far as Betty was concerned but, though I felt the same, there was a war to be fought and we were trained fighter pilots. This was the beginning of the end, and as we all climbed into our Hurricanes having bid our 'adieus' that fine September day, I wondered how many of us would see Usworth or Newcastle again. Strange as it may seem, dirty, smoky, old Newcastle was to us seventh heaven when compared with the rolling green fields of southern England.

We arrived, however, at a completely blitzed aerodrome where we were greeted by the remnants of 43 Squadron: some on crutches, others with an arm in a sling, and yet another, who had had his face torn apart by an exploding cannon shell, with a head swathed in bandages. Though they had suffered so many casualties it was quite amazing to see them walking about. Needless to say they were very pleased to see us, having just been up on the third sortie that day and were still waiting for news of the latest casualties.

We only had time to re-fuel when we were called out on an operational trip that evening. There was no interception, however, and no casualties. The next morning, to my great disappointment, I was not called upon to fly and later the Squadron went off. In the event I was the more fortunate, as of 12 Hurricanes six were shot down. Three officers were killed and three sergeants wounded. Amongst the casualties were Stuart Parnall, my best friend, Scotty and the young South African George Drake. They were all lovely people, just like Alex Obelenski and 'Ching' Mackenzie, with whom I would have flown to hell, if necessary, in glorious comradeship.

With little experience, 607 Squadron had arrived at one of the 'hottest'

Sector Stations at an extremely busy time. Without time to adjust to or train for the new operational conditions, it was inevitable that the lethal 109s would harshly treat the 'County of Durham' Hurricanes. Yet again, this RAF squadron, new to the fray, went on patrol flying a useless formation, and paid the price. As ever, the 109s had the advantage of height, sun, and used the excellent Schwarm tactical formation. This divided each Staffel into three sections of four aircraft that flew in line abreast, but the aircraft were well spread out so that there was no fear of collision. In the event of combat, the Schwarm would split into two fighting pairs of leader and wingman, the Rotte, so the fundamental principals were both flexibility and mutual support. It would not be until the 1941 'season' that Fighter Command grasped the benefits of and copied this enemy tactic.

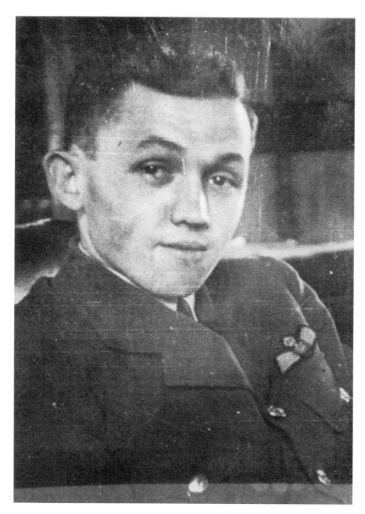

The South African, Pilot Officer George Drake.

Somehow we could not believe it. No one talked about it and we all hoped for news to filter through from some remote pub or perhaps a hospital. No news came, so we hardened ourselves to the worst: 'Killed in Action'. We bit back our tears and our sorrow. It was "You heard about Stuart and Scotty? Rotten luck, wasn't it?" Someone would add "And young George, bloody good blokes all of them". After that epitaph the mater would be dismissed with the ordering of another round of drinks to avoid any trace of further sentiment.

Another problem faced by the auxiliaries was that losses did, in fact, affect personnel deeply given that these units were all locally raised. As a result, old school and family friends, business associates, even relatives, all served together. Casualties understandably had a depressing effect on these units.

By September 17th, 23-year old Pilot Officer Harry Welford was a veteran. On that day 'B' Flight scrambled at 1505 hours on the Squadron's fourth sortie of the day, Harry flying Blue 2. On this occasion the six Hurricanes patrolled the Biggin Hill/Gravesend line at 17,000 feet. Between 1500 and 1600 hours, a multi-wave massed enemy fighter sweep crossed the South Coast. Each wave comprised two Gruppen of 109s (some 60 fighters). Suddenly, 'B' Flight was bounced from above and behind by a horde of 109s.

When attacked we were warned to break formation. I broke and took evasive action, as a result of which I lost the Squadron. As we had instructions to re-form rather than fly alone, I saw a large group of fighters ahead, which I then intended to join up with until I realised that they were Me 109s! I fired a quick burst at them, but an unseen 109 fired at me and hit by air intake with a cannon shell. I did a quick flick roll that dropped me below cloud. No 109s about but a lone Hurricane that guarded my tail as I forced landed. The engine had seized and looking down I saw a field in which I thought I could land. As I approached, glycol and smoke streamed from the engine. When I opened the hood, these fumes were sucked through the cockpit and impaired my vision. The field was actually smaller than I thought, but there was a wattle fence that acted like a carrier's arrester hook. The plane then skidded across the second field but was brought to an abrupt halt by a tree at the far end, cracking my head on the reflector sight. Blood poured down my face, and thinking that the plane might catch fire I undid my straps and jumped out, only to fall flat on my face because my leg, which had been wounded by shrapnel, collapsed on me. Two farm workers rushed over and picked me up, putting me on a section of wattle fence. They told me that there was a German plane in the next field with the pilot in it, very dead. I regret now that I declined their offer to show me, but at the time I felt pretty dicky.

In hospital I gave my report to our flight commander, Flight Lieutenant Jim Bazin who acknowledged that I had shot down the 109 in the field next to where my Hurricane crashed. Now, however, I am not so sure as we have not been able to identity a potential candidate from the German crashes that day. Anyway, I was thereafter in hospital for a while with 'Tubby' Badger, 43 Squadron's former CO, who was very brave, always laughing. Sadly, he ultimately succumbed to his wounds, which was a great shame, as he was a fine man.

Research into this combat suggests that Harry was shot down by Hauptmann Eduard Neumann, Gruppenkommandeur of I/JG 27. The German's logbook confirms that he shot down two Hurricanes during this action, the other probably being 607 Squadron's Sergeant Landesdell, who was killed. Neumann was very experienced, having fought in the Spanish Civil War, and later became Kommodore of JG 27, which went to North Africa in 1941. There one of Neumann's pilots became one of the most incredibly successful fighter pilots of all time: Hans-Joachim Marseille, the 'Star of Africa'. Ultimately, Neumann's personal victory tally was 13, and he later became leader of the German fighter forces in Italy.

Both Harry Welford and Eduard Neumann survived the war. The former re-joined 607 Squadron on October 20th, 1940, by which time the unit had been withdrawn to Turnhouse, in Scotland. During the Battle of Britain, 607 Squadron had lost nine pilots killed. For the next two months, Harry passed on his combat experience to replacement pilots before being posted away to be an instructor. He would not return to operations until November 1944, flying Spitfire Mk IXs with 222 Squadron and by which time the air war had changed significantly.

Soon after the war, Squadron Leader Harry Welford left the service, and at the time of our first contact, back in the mid-1980s, was living in comfortable retirement, with his Betty, on the Devonshire coast. We enjoyed voluminous correspondence and several meetings before

Harry's passing in 1996. Sadly, as time marches ever on, the Few get fewer.

Squadron Leader Harry Welford at a Ramrod event, Worcester Guildhall, 1995. Sadly he died the following year.

Chapter Thirteen

Corporal Fred Roberts

LAC Fred Roberts. The frame was made from the tip of a crashed 19 Squadron Spitfire.

On September 21st, 1940, official photographers descended on Fowlmere airfield and recorded on film the activity to hand. These photographs, largely featuring Squadron Leader Brian Lane's resident 19 Squadron, are now preserved by the Imperial War Museum and are available to all. Consequently many have been used as representative illustrations in countless books. Invariably however, unless the author or book packager is informed, the photographs are given general captions, such as 'Spitfire pilots at rest', without identifying the unit or personnel concerned.

One of the most widely used of these photographs shows Sergeant Bernard 'Jimmy' Jennings sat in the cockpit of Spitfire X4474, 'QVI', whilst an anonymous armourer attends to the 'plumbing', and an equally anonymous rigger attends to the pilot. It was with both surprise and pleasure, therefore, that, after publication of my first book, *Spitfire Squadron* (Air Research Publications, 1990), which featured the story of 19 Squadron 1939-41, and in which included the photograph in question, I was contacted by the armourer concerned. Incredibly he, Fred Roberts, had never seen the photograph before, despite its wide use! Fred and his wife Mary lived in South Wales, but by coincidence had lived in Worcester, my hometown. for many years after the war. So began an enduring friendship, throughout which we have been delighted to welcome Fred and Mary Roberts at just about every event we have staged since our first contact.

In September 1992, at the launch of *The Invisible Thread*, we arranged the static display of an RAF Exhibition Flight Spitfire Mk XVI, painted to represent X4474. So it was that 52 years later, Wing Commander 'Jimmy' Jennings and Fred Roberts were reunited with 'QV-I'. Jimmy drew the line at climbing into the cockpit, however, so our recreation of the famous photograph featured the pair posing adjacent to the Spitfire. It was in the nick of time, as sadly Jimmy died a few years later.

When a 'new' personality appears on the scene, one of the first tasks is to document their experiences, as was the case with Fred Roberts. As a member of the essential but less glamorised support staff, his story offers both a refreshing and fascinating insight into the working lives of those who also served.

> Jimmy Belton and myself joined 19 Squadron in July 1939, as 'rookie' armourers straight from our six-month course at Manby. Full of enthusiasm and expecting to see Spitfires everywhere, we arrived at Duxford to find everything quiet and more or less closed for the weekend. Of course this was still the 'strawberries and cream and fruitcake for tea' period enjoyed by the pre-war RAF, which was like a posh flying club.
>
> On Sunday, September 3rd, 1939, several armament personnel of both 19 and 66 Squadrons, myself included, spent the day transporting ammunition from railway wagons in Whittlesford Yard to the Duxford ammunition store. None of the aircraft were yet armed, however. Whilst we worked in the yard, evacuee trains passed by. The landlord of the nearby pub called us in to listen to Mr Chamberlain's speech, he took us into the snug with a free pint. After the Prime Minister's announcement, the air raid warning sirens sounded and our 19 Squadron

was scrambled. We all thought 'They won't shoot much down with empty ammo boxes!'

From thereon the Armament Section was kept very busy as we had to re-sight the Browning machine-guns to work with the new reflector sights. When I had arrived at Duxford some of the Spitfires still had the old ring and bead sight. We also repeatedly practised re-arming until two armourers and assistants could change all eight ammo tanks, cock all guns and replace all panels in about three minutes flat.

It was early January 1940 when one of 66 Squadron's Spitfires, N3036, was hit by return fire whilst attacking a raider off the Norfolk coast, and made a wheels-up forced landing on the cliff tops near Cromer. We had to go out and unload the eight guns. We couldn't take out the ammo tanks because of the wings resting on the ground, so we had to stay and guard the plane until it was removed later that night.

At Duxford it was routine work, daily inspections etc. Early in February 1940, Douglas Bader, having resumed his RAF career, joined 19 Squadron. His first flight was in the Squadron Magister, and he proceeded to beat up the aerodrome in every imaginable way. It was memorable! He will also be remembered for taking the roof off the old peacetime cricket pavilion when he hit it upon landing, removing the tailwheel of his Spitfire in the process.

Fowlmere, September 21ˢᵗ, 1940. Sergeant Bernard 'Jimmy' Jennings DFM in the 'office', Fred Roberts attending the guns (Imperial War Museum).

On February 29th, 1940, some of the armourers, including myself, along with flight fitters and riggers, were detailed to travel by lorry to Whittlesford village where one of our Spitfires, flown by Pilot Officer Trenchard, had crashed during a night flight. The plane was in a thousand pieces. I remember one oleo leg and wheel a quarter of a mile away with a belt of ammo around it. The engine lay in a crater about five feet deep, the cockpit in bits around it. I still have the tip of one of this Spitfire's propellers, which I had made into a picture frame. This prop tip I recovered from the Duxford aircraft graveyard a few days after the crash.

On May 25th, 19 Squadron moved to Hornchurch to participate in the air operation covering the Dunkirk evacuation. It was a very hard 10 days there, up and on Readiness at 0500 or 0530, and remaining on duty until nightfall when the last gun had been cleaned and the final panel replaced on the aircraft. Waiting was the worst. It was all strange to us knowing that the Spitfires were actually going into action. The question foremost in our minds was 'who will return?' One good thing about Hornchurch was that we met up again with the lads of 222 Squadron, with whom we had previously shared Duxford.

Throughout the entire war, the most badly shot up aircraft I ever saw was whilst we were at Hornchurch. It was Eric Ball's. I remember Douglas Bader and his wife, Thelma, coming over from the 222v Squadron dispersal (as he was by then a flight commander with that squadron), and together the three of them counted the bullet holes.

At Duxford, where the old Watch Tower had stood, there had been erected on the Station Flight and Cambridge University Air Squadron hangar a sandbag protected machine-gun post. On one particular morning it was manned by 'Ginger' Hunt, one of 19 Squadron's Armourer Assistants. In 19 Squadron's hangar stood a fully armed Spitfire, guns all loaded and cocked, hangar doors open. By coincidence the gunsight was roughly aligned with the machine-gun post. 'Pickles', one of our Maintenance Flight armourers, who actually did the office work, was detailed to instruct a new member of the Section, a boy entrant, on the Spitfire's layout and procedures. Whilst giving this instruction he sat in the cockpit whilst the trainee stood on the wing root. "To fire the guns, young lad, you turn this ring and press this button", which Pickles did. As the eight guns fired, from inside the hangar the noise was terrific! Fortunately the gunner on the Station Flight hangar roof was not physically hurt, but he was pretty shaken and there were a few punctured sandbags!

On June 25th, we moved a few miles down the Royston Road, and a mile up the country road, to Fowlmere. The airfield was on a hilltop and was Duxford's satellite, codenamed G1. When we arrived the farmer was bringing in the crop, so to speed things up some of us were detailed to help, whilst others erected tents etc. Living conditions were rough, but fortunately the weather was good, which helped.

It was between 8-8.30 am on August 31st, when the first bombs were dropped. We, the ground staff, were queuing for breakfast, the squadron's Spitfires being airborne. We heard the noise of what transpired to be Do 17s approaching. I dived into the nearest slit trench and upon looking up could see the sun shining on little dots high in the sky. I could also see the first stick of bombs falling. Fortunately they were released too late and so only two fell on the airfield, one amongst the bell tents making a crater about four feet deep and five feet across. The earth blown out of the crater collapsed one of the tents. There were two lads asleep inside who were partially buried, but neither was harmed. The second bomb exploded near the boundary fence, but the rest of that stick fell in the orchards and watercress beds beyond the airfield. We had permission to collect as many bombed apples as we wanted. Looking back now it makes me smile to think of myself and others crouching in that trench holding enamel plates over our heads with cutlery and mugs in hand!

I also recall that we had Flight Sergeant George 'Grumpy' Unwin's 'A' Flight Spitfire up on trestles in the blister hangar when a scramble came. He came running along with the other pilots, but due to his aircraft being indisposed, was unable to take-off with the others. He was yelling and swearing for his plane, and I reckon that we broke the record for returning a Spitfire to serviceability! George was airborne and after the others just 10 minutes later following a straight take-off from the hangar across wind and with no engine warm-up. It certainly showed the courage of the man and the faith he placed in his groundcrew.

There were always excellent relations between 19 Squadron's ground staff and aircrew. The pre-war regular officers were real gentlemen in their dealings with us and acknowledged the fact that we looked up to them as responsible people. The regular NCO pilots were much closer to us, having been through the ranks themselves, and were excellent people to work with, men like George Unwin, Harry Steere and Jack Potter. Many others followed on, who were also good, especially the

Czechs, but they were sometimes a little impatient. Some of the young commissioned pilots who joined the Squadron in 1940 did not appear to have the same character or confidence as the pre-war officers and seemed to be stand-offish. Reflecting on this in my old age, I think that really they were shy of us, we being the old hands.

I felt that the aircrew all fully appreciated our efforts to keep the Squadron at as high a pitch of efficiency as was possible, at all times and often under difficult conditions. We o the ground certainly had our favourites amongst the pilots, mine being Squadron Leader Brian Lane DFC and Flight Sergeant 'Grumpy George' Unwin DFM. I suppose it was because I looked after their armament that they became personal to me.

In October 1940 it was with great regret that I was posted from 19 Squadron to 151 Squadron at Digby. I missed the camaraderie of 19, but although I asked to return, my request fell on deaf ears.

Today, Fred Roberts is intensely proud of the time he spent on the front line with 19 Squadron during the Battle of Britain, and is another enthusiastic visitor to air shows and museums. Those visits are always nostalgic, often moving. As Fred says, "On my annual visit to the RAF Museum at Hendon, I always stand and look at the Spitfire with a tear in my eye."

53 years later, Wing Commander Jennings and Fred Roberts reunited with 'Spitfire QV-I' at a Ramrod book launch.

Chapter Fourteen

Sergeant Jack Stokoe

Sergeant Jack Stokoe, his top-button undone in classic fighter pilot pose.

During my research into Spitfire R6644, the aircraft safely abandoned by Pilot Officer Franek Surma near Malvern on May 11th, 1941, I was able to identify many pilots who had also flown this machine, and record their stories. The Spitfire concerned was taken on charge by No 5 OTU at Aston Down on June 6th, 1940, remaining there until damaged in a landing accident on July 4th. Reading the list of young pilots posted to Aston Down for Spitfire training is like reading a roll call of the lost, for so many went on to perish either in the Battle of Britain or later in the war. Names such as Richard Hillary, Ray Aeberhardt, Eddy Egan, Gerald Maffett, Colin Francis, Robert Dewey, Noel Agazarian, Peter Pease, the list goes ever on and on.

Amongst those who flew R6644 and survived was Jack Stokoe, from Berwick, East Lothian, who reported for duty at Aston Down on June 10th. With him were Colin Francis and Eddy Egan, both of whom would remain 'Missing in Action' until their bodies were recovered by enthusiasts long after the war, and Don Kingaby, who went on to become an extremely successful fighter ace dubbed the '109 specialist'. In total,

38 young pilots arrived for instruction with Sergeant Stokoe and his friends, and all were posted to operational fighter squadrons just 13 days later. This gives some idea of the volume of pilots processed by the OTUs during 1940 in an effort to maintain Dowding's squadrons at full strength.

In 1992, Jack was amongst those pilots who kindly signed our print to raise money for the Surma Memorial Trust for Youth. Mark Postlethwaite and I enjoyed several fine summer days travelling the country collecting the signatures of certain pilots unable to attend the actual Great Malvern launch. We visited Ludwik Martel, 'Bertie' Wootten, Sir Denis Crowley-Milling, David Scott-Malden, and Jack Stokoe, to literally name but a few. We found Jack's house, eventually, in the wilds of north Kent, and there we recorded the following interview:-

Only a year before the Battle of Britain began, my contemporaries and I were pursuing our civilian careers whilst learning to fly with the RAF VR in our spare time. The majority of us were 18-19 years old. Being aircrew, when called up in September 1939, we were automatically given the rank of sergeant, which at first caused some dismay amongst the ranks of professional sergeants, many of whom had taken 20 years to reach that exulted rank!

Most of us had only 50-60 hours flying on elementary types like Tiger Moths and Magisters when we were called up. After a brief spell at ITW to instil some discipline into us, we had about 100 hours on Harvards at FTS, which included a few trips actually firing guns. We were then posted to an OTU, in my case Aston Down, before being posted to an operational fighter squadron with just 10-15 hours on Spitfires recorded in our logbooks.

After training I was posted to 263 Squadron, which had first flown Gladiators, then Hurricanes, and was now converting to twin-engined Westland Whirlwinds. I chose to remain on singles, however, and so was posted to 603 'City of Edinburgh' Squadron, based at Dyce in Scotland. There were only three of us NCO pilots, the rest being officers, mostly auxiliaries.

By August 27th, 1940, we had moved to Hornchurch, just north of the Thames Estuary, by which time I had about 70 hours on Spits and was therefore most fortunate. I could have gone straight to a front line fighter squadron from OTU, as indeed so many pilots did, and if so I would not have rated my chances of survival very highly. I had even already seen, but not actually engaged, two German reconnaissance bombers over northern Scotland.

On August 29th, we flew four patrols, intercepting Me 109s on two of them. I claimed one damaged but the trimming wires of my own aircraft were shot away. The following day we made four more interceptions, during the course of which I was credited with having destroyed an Me 109 and damaged another. Again, however, my own aircraft was damaged, by a cannon-shell in the windscreen, and my hand was slightly cut by splinters. On September 1st came three more interceptions of 20 plus bandits, one of which I shot down in flames over Canterbury.

On September 2nd, I was involved with two more interceptions, during the course of which I damaged two enemy aircraft but was myself shot down in flames, fortunately baling out. On that occasion, as I was attacking an enemy aircraft I remember machine-gun bullets, or maybe cannon shells, hitting my Spitfire, followed by flames in the cockpit as the petrol tanks exploded. I thought "Christ! I've got to get out of here and *quick*!" I undid the straps and opened the hood, but this turned the flames into a blowtorch. I was not wearing gloves, as during our hasty scramble I had forgotten them, but had to put my hands back into the fire to invert the Spitfire so that I could drop out (no ejector seats in those days!). I remember seeing sheets of skin peeling off the backs of my hands before I fell out of the aeroplane. I was then concerned regarding whether the parachute would function or whether it had been damaged by fire, but I pulled the ripcord and fortunately it opened perfectly.

I landed in a field, but the Home Guard queried whether I was an enemy agent! A few choice words in English soon convinced them I was genuine, and thereafter I was rushed into the emergency hospital at Leeds Castle, suffering from shock and severe burns to my hands, neck and face.

I was in hospital for six weeks before returning to operational duties on October 22nd, with further combat successes. A second tour of duty with 54 Squadron followed, which included a second bale out (over the sea!). I was then seconded to a training unit but returned to ops, flying fighters, later in the war.

The point about the incident when I was shot down over Kent on September 2ⁿᵈ, 1940 is that at the time 603 Squadron was suffering such heavy casualties that that administration got pretty chaotic. For four days after baling out, although quite safe in hospital, I was officially posted 'Missing in Action'!

During the war, Jack destroyed a total of seven German aircraft and was awarded the DFC. Retiring from the service as a Squadron Leader in 1946, in 'civvy street' he became a trading standards officer. We attended a number of events in Southeast England together, including the Biggin Hill air show in 2,000, at which Jack was able to meet German Battle of Britain veteran and author Ulrich Steinhilper. Sadly, Jack died soon afterwards, and so passed another one-time courageous and dedicated pilot who had fought for his country during its hour of greatest need.

Squadron Leader Jack Stokoe DFC and Dilip Sarkar at Biggin Hill, 1998.
Sadly, Jack died soon afterwards. (*Andrew Long*)

Chapter Fifteen

LAC Ray Johnson

During the Great War, 152 'Hyderabad' Squadron had seen action but was disbanded in 1919. The Squadron then re-formed, at Acklington, on October 2nd, 1939, and was initially equipped with obsolete Gladiator biplanes, which were fortunately exchanged for Spitfires in December. On July 12th, 1940, the Squadron flew south to Warmwell, near the Dorset seaside resort of Weymouth, in 10 Group. Flying therefrom, 152 Squadron's main responsibility was to defend the RN base at Portland. When the Squadron moved south, 19-year old Ray Johnson, an armourer, was amongst an advance party of personnel flown down from Acklington in a Handley Page Harrow transport aircraft. Now 81, Ray remembers:-

> Warmwell was a grass airfield not far from the Army camp at Bovingdon, and actually adjacent to the spot where the famous 'Lawrence of Arabia' was killed on his motorcycle. Our new airfield was not a Sector Station but a pre-war practice camp used during firing exercises at nearby Lulworth Cove. Upon arrival we operated from the concrete apron in front of the hangars, but a week or so later the Station Commander called us all together and said something to the effect of this: "One of these days in the not too distant future the Hun will appear

152 Squadron's groundcrew indicating the prevailing British spirit of 1940!

over those Purbeck Hills and knock three kinds of shit out of us! Therefore 152 Squadron will disperse to the far side of the airfield to thus ensure that as little damage as possible will occur. The hangar is only to be used for major inspections and repairs." He was right about the probability of us getting hit, as we were several times, but luckily not as badly as those in 11 Group.

Our duties were to defend not only Portland but also Southampton and the Westland Aircraft Factory at Yeovil. There were certainly hectic days ahead, during which we were at dispersal from dawn to dusk. It seemed as though we were always at Readiness. Re-arming, re-fuelling and daily inspections of our Spitfires seemed to follow on without pause. It was certainly thrilling to see 'your' aircraft return with its gun ports in the leading edges open and black streaks down the undersides indicating that it had been in action. Very often there was a victory roll before the pilot lowered the undercarriage and landed. Sometimes, though, your aircraft did not return, leaving you wondering what had happened. Sometimes a badly shot up Spitfire would land, like when Flight Lieutenant 'Bottle' Boitel-Gill crashed right in a corner of our airfield. His Spitfire was absolutely riddled. We counted over 70 holes, that is points of entry, and thereafter lost count! 'Bottle' was one of those unflappable types, he never rushed, always appeared casual. He was a veteran cigarette smoker, using the long cigarette holder that he always carried. This time, after alighting from the wreck, he calmly placed a fag into the holder and said "I thought that I had better put this in the corner, out of the way"! As I have said, he was a very cool cookie.

Another time, Flying Officer Graham 'Cocky' Cox landed with his head and shoulders protruding above the cockpit, his seat supports having collapsed either due to enemy action or violent evasive manoeuvres. The seat was resting on the elevator and rudder controls!

Flying Officer 'Jumbo' Deansley was another who had a lucky escape, two in fact, twice crashing into the sea and being rescued both times. He later became a night fighter pilot, survived the war but died recently.

One day we saw a formation of a dozen or so twin-engined aircraft approaching at 8-10,000 feet, and drop their bombloads on us. It was all over in a matter of minutes. They were pretty accurate. The hangar and a number of aircraft were destroyed or damaged, and delayed action

Flight Lieutenant Derek 'Bottle' Boitle-Gill DFC.

bombs kept exploding periodically over the next couple of days. There were a number of casualties amongst ground personnel. As practically all our waking hours were spent at dispersal, at the wooded end of the airfield, for years afterwards in any panic the standard cry was "Away to the woods!"

On another occasion, towards the end of that long, hot summer, half a dozen of us were having a snack in the canteen run by the WRVS, which had better food than the NAAFI, when a lone enemy aircraft bombed and strafed the camp at zero feet. It was a day of particularly poor visibility and I remember diving under one of the heavy hardwood tables, which were standard equipment in those days. A radiator from the heating system landed on top of it, again, some were luckier than others.

A sad loss during the Battle of Britain was 21-year old Pilot Officer Douglas Shepley, who had only been married for six weeks. His elder brother, a Flight Lieutenant, had already been lost over Dunkirk. His sister, a nurse, had been lost at sea when the *SS Lancastrian* was bombed and sunk. His family lived at Woodthorpe Hall, near Sheffield, and his wife, 'Biddy', and his parents funded the purchase of a Spitfire in Doug's memory. To this day there is a pub near Woodthorpe Hall called 'The Shepley Spitfire'.

During the summer of 1940, the invasion of this country was more than a distinct possibility. The pros and cons and whys and wherefores have been voiced and written about many times elsewhere, so I will not go into all that here, but suffice to say that the possibility eventually receded, and as the day's shortened so did daylight aerial activity. We were then able to have a bit of time off, so trips were arranged into neighbouring seaside towns Weymouth and Bournemouth. During the evenings we would visit pubs closer to the camp, such as those at Woodsford, Puddletown, Broadmaine and Dorchester. The pilots had their haunts, we had ours, although occasionally our paths would cross, such as at the Gloucester Hotel in Weymouth. It was a very heavy night indeed, and a number of us had to have a whiff of oxygen for breakfast!

Ray remained with 152 Squadron throughout the war, serving overseas in Burma and India. Today, he is an active member of the 152 Squadron Association, and his 80th birthday party was well attended by survivors. As Ray said, they "had a great time remembering the time of their lives!"

We have enjoyed Ray's company at many events, such as those staged by Ramrod at Duxford, Yeovil and Worcester, and his great sense of humour only serves to increase his popularity. Indeed, and as Ray delights in telling, I laughed my socks off listening to the recordings of his wartime experiences when painting my soon-to-be-born daughters bedroom!

Ray Johnson pictured recently at the RAF Coningsby with a BBMF Spitfire, PS915, carrying the colours of 152 Squadron from Far East wartime days.

Chapter Sixteen

Pilot Officer Keith Lawrence

In addition to the British and free pilots from the occupied lands who fought in 1940, we must also remember those from the Commonwealth who came to help fight our 'forest fire'. For example, 4,000 New Zealanders served with the RAF during the Second World War; many perished, but Keith Ashley Lawrence numbers amongst the survivors.

Born on November 25th, 1919, and educated at Invercargill, Keith applied to join the regular RAF via the Direct Entry Commonwealth Recruiting Scheme in 1938. In March 1939, therefore, he joined a contingent of 'Kiwis' sent to train with the RAF in England. Afterwards, in November, he was granted a Short Service Commission and posted to 234 Squadron. At that time, 234 was equipped with the Bristol Blenheim, but exchanged these for the much more exciting Spitfire in March 1940.

During the Battle of Britain, 234 Squadron served throughout with 10 Group, initially at St Eval, flying from where Pilot Officer Lawrence opened his account of enemy aircraft destroyed, then at Middle Wallop from August 14th onwards. As opposed to the situation between 11 and 12 Groups, there was an excellent spirit of co-operation between 11 and 10 Groups, and so it was that 11 Group frequently called upon 10 Group's squadrons to assist with interceptions over the capital and Southeast. On September 7th, 234 Squadron was scrambled to assist in the defence of London, and on that day Keith was credited with having destroyed an Me 109 and damaged a Do 17. Two days later, however, 234 returned to St Eval, in Cornwall, but Keith was posted to 603 Squadron at Hornchurch. On September 15th, he destroyed an Me 109 and damaged two more. The young New Zealander was not to remain there long, however, as Keith himself now relates:-

On October 8th, 1940, and at the instigation of the Prime Minister, No 421 Flight was formed at Gravesend. Known as the 'Jim Crow Flight', the unit had been formed largely from a detached flight of 66 Squadron, and was equipped with the new Spitfire Mk II, but included pilots from throughout Fighter Command who had fought in the Battle of Britain. Posted to the unit upon formation, I found that our purpose, flying singly or in pairs, was to report on the movement of enemy shipping in the Channel, or the build-up of *Luftwaffe* formations. Conjecture is that here was cover to permit ULTRA secrets to be used to best advantage but without giving the game away.

The proposed German invasion of England was called off on October 12th, and the Battle of Britain officially ended on October 31st. There was no respite however, and in fact, for the fighter forces of either side, which continued to engage over the South Coast until the weather really closed in during early 1941. Indeed, so far as November and December 1940 were concerned, they have rightly been called the 'Forgotten Months' (a book by John Foreman, Air Research Publications, 1989).

By November 1940, we were stationed at RAF Hawkinge, on the high ground above the Straits of Dover. The Flight's first daily task was for a single Spitfire to fly a weather patrol along the Kentish coast between North Foreland and Dungeness to obtain met 'actuals' on the cloud conditions and formations. At the same time we would listen out for any operational instructions from Control. The pilot detailed for the weather flight would take off between first light and sunrise.

On the morning of November 27th, I get airborne into a cloudy sky and fly uneventfully northeastwards to North Foreland and then turn 180 degrees at about 8,000 feet in the direction of Dungeness. There being nothing on the R/T to warn or distract, I cannot but be aware of the beauty, loneliness and apparent peacefulness which one experiences when flying between layers of cloud at that height, moe so in the half light preceding sunrise. With not a sound in my headphones, but on constant lookout, I head towards Deal, still at 8,000 feet, and flying above some 5/10 stratocu and with 10/10 cu and stratocu overhead.

Suddenly, one corner of that scene turns from tranquillity to action, in a second! There, slightly on my port side, 500 feet below, through a gap in the cloud and streaking eastwards towards France, are three Me 109s in fairly close formation! At that speed not a second to lose, full throttle, stuff the nose down, switch on reflector sight and draw a bead. I start firing, three, maybe four seconds. An instant later I am falling earthwards in my stocking feet, slightly to my right I glimpse the rotating wing of my aircraft, falling as if a leaf. Come on now, get things in the right order! Parachute, 'D' ring on left-hand side, so reach across for it with right hand. Right hand won't move. Try assisting right hand with left hand…. I am still falling (presumably by this time at terminal velocity, 120 mph) so must get a move on. I scrabble around with my left hand, trying to get at the left-sided release handle that will release my chute.

Success! The proverbial sigh of relief cut short as I realise that I am fast drifting in a westerly wind over the coast and out to a sea capped with white waves. Minutes later I am plunged into the cold, cold sea of late November, about a mile from land. With my right arm useless I must, left-handed, find the tube with which to inflate my life jacket, unbuckle my parachute harness and somehow keep my head above water. Within minutes I am coughing, spluttering, choking, and swallowing much seawater. The parachute shroud lines are everywhere, like a web. The Mae West does not inflate, its bladder evidently split by the ejection force on my Sutton harness, which supposedly holds the pilot firmly in the cockpit. With just the use of one arm and one leg, it seems that I am losing, engulfed in the cold wateriness that I cannot rise above.

Suddenly what seems like a high dark wall is looming over me, from which extends an arm of great strength to haul me bodily onto a boat manned by sailors of the Royal Navy.

Thereafter Keith, a lucky man indeed, was treated at Ramsgate Hospital with a fractured right leg, lacerated left leg and dislocated right shoulder. A week later he was transferred 90 miles west, 'most painfully and by an ambulance with solid tyres', to RAF Hospital Halton. It would be a year before Keith was considered fully recovered and fit enough to resume operational flying duties.

This simple recounting of an experience which was not unique, and befell many a pilot or other aircrew during wartime, tells but part of the story behind the announcement in the newspapers or on the radio, 'One of our aircraft was lost today', its background and consequences, one or two of which I now add as a footnote.

On the morning of this episode, my arrival at the airfield dispersal hut, being slightly less than punctual (as is the wont of some!), I just grabbed the first life jacket to hand. At that time, not all Mae Wests had been modified by the addition of a fluorescein dye packet. Fortunately the example that I picked up had been. My RN rescuers later told me that they first steered to my still inflated parachute, blowing across the surface, but on reaching it found no body. Only then, some distance away, did they sight my life-saving patch of bright fluorescent green seawater.

Also, many years later, when this escapade had become just another event in my distant past, I became aware of a group of aviation archaeologists who were trying to locate the remains of my Spitfire, which had apparently crashed near Finglesham, two miles north-west of Deal. By talking to the village's older inhabitants myself, I was able to ascertain that my crashing aircraft had caused no injury or loss of life.

Curiosity mounting, I decided to research for information about the sortie flown by the four German fighters that morning, November 27th, 1940. The Dover Post of the Royal Observer Corps entry for 0700 hours that morning read 'Hostile heard'. Was my assailant one of a regular dawn patrol flown by a German *Schwarm* over Kent? The answer to this question may well lie in the archives of the 'Y' Service, the intelligence unit that intercepted all enemy R/T transmissions. These transcripts, however, are closed to the public.

Be that as it may, available from German combat reports we do know that I was the victim of *Oberleutnant* Gustav 'Mickey' Sprick,

Oberleutnant Gustav 'Mickey' Sprick.

Staffelkapitän of 8/JG 26. He had been amongst the first German fighter pilots with 20 aerial victories and received his Knight's Cross accordingly on October 1st, 1940. On June 28th, 1941, the wing of his Me 109F collapsed during a dogfight over France, and he was killed in the resulting crash. Sprick's final tally was 31 victories.

After recovery and a Spitfire refresher course, I again made close acquaintance with JG 26 when I was posted to Malta. Based in Sicily, German bombers attacked Malta several times a day, their fighter escort often being provided by 7/JG 26.

What would have made the perfect postscript to this adventure for me would have been discovery of my Royal Navy rescuers and their ship. So this has so far not proved possible, but I give thanks, as must many other of my fellow pilots of those days.

After serving on Malta, Keith Lawrence was awarded the DFC, and he later flew dive-bombing sorties against German V2 rocket launching sites on the Dutch coast. After the war, he returned to his native New Zealand, serving as an Air Traffic Controller in the Territorial Air Force. Later, he returned to England and a new life in Sussex, but is now enjoying a peaceful retirement with his wife, Kay, in the West Country.

Keith and Kay Lawrence have also been both regular and welcome guests at various Ramrod events at Worcester and elsewhere. Despite his impressive wartime record, however, or perhaps even because of it, it is difficult to get Keith to talk openly of his experiences. Indeed, persuading him to contribute these notes was not an easy task! He is one of those people who is a good listener, but in the great tradition of the time, will never be found 'shooting a line'. Personally however, and as with all of the veterans mentioned in this book, it has been a real privilege to have entertained Mr & Mrs Keith Lawrence DFC, although I know that he will hate me saying it!

Keith Lawrence DFC, an 'ace' from New Zealand, at a Ramrod book launch.

Chapter Seventeen

Vignettes: 1

The following quotes have been selected randomly, mainly from personal correspondence but occasionally from records now in the public domain. In 'Vignettes: 1' we are looking at the situation leading up to the Battle of Britain, and in '2' the Battle of Britain proper. That having been said there is no intention to comprehensively describe the events in question, just a matter of providing some atmospheric first-hand accounts with which to conclude our presentation.

Air Chief Marshal Sir Hugh Dowding:-

I must therefore request that as a matter of paramount urgency the Air Ministry will consider and decide what level of strength is to be left to Fighter Command for the defence of this country, and will assure me that when this level has been reached, not one fighter will be sent across the Channel, however urgent and insistent appeals for help may be.

I believe that, if an adequate fighter force is kept in this country, if the fleets remain in being, and if the Home Forces are suitably organised to resist invasion, we should be able to carry on the war single handed for some time, if not indefinitely. But, if the Home Defence Force is drained away in desperate attempts to remedy the situation in France, defeat in France will involve the final, complete and irremediable defeat of this country.

Flying Officer 'Bunny' Currant DFC:-

In May 1940, 605 Squadron was based at Wick, in Scotland, but on the 21st we flew south, to Hawkinge, just inland of Folkestone and the closest RAF station to France. From there we were to fly daily patrols over France to supplement the hard-pressed squadrons of the AASF. On that day, I was ordered to patrol Arras with Flying Officer Hope as my Number Two. As we prepared to take off, Squadron Leader Teddy Donaldson, the CO of 151 Squadron, landed from his patrol over France and was rather pessimistic about the outlook over there. From Hawkinge I could see smoke on the horizon over France and could hear the rumble of distant bombs.

Wing Commander 'Bunny' Currant DSO DFC at a Ramrod event in Great Malvern, 1993.

We took off and climbed, heading for the scene of battle so clearly visible as we flew south. At about 15,000 feet over Arras, I saw an He 111 dropping bombs, saw them explode along the road and in some woods as I opened the throttle and dived. Gunsight on, straps tight and locked firm as I raced in with a quarter deflection from behind. Got the 111 well in the sight and opened fire. Saw hits on the port engine and fuselage. Smoke, steam and flames appeared and it banked left in a fairly steep dive. The next thing was extraordinary. I saw and heard no enemy fire striking my aircraft but suddenly there was silence as the engine seized, the propeller stopped. There it was, in front of my nose, a stationary airscrew! The cockpit filled with fumes, hissing noisily. Steam and glycol but no smoke. I opened the hood, undid my straps and climbed out onto the wing, intending to jump. I then did a very stupid thing: I changed my mind, which said "I can put this Hurricane down". So I climbed back in and glided down, and with wheels up slid into a field. As I had no time to do up my straps, as the aircraft skidded rapidly to a sudden stop, I hit the side of the cockpit and broke my nose, cutting my face. I clambered out and looked up to see Flying Officer Hope circling overhead before flying off back to Hawkinge.

I grabbed my maps, parachute and Sidcot flying suit before making my way to a farmhouse where the folk very kindly bathed my cuts and we conversed quite ineffectively in pidgin French and English. I was aware, however, of them pointing eastwards and could distinguish amongst the gabble of French words "Les salle Boches", which I assumed meant 'the bloody Germans'. Naturally I was eager to head for Calais and get a boat back to England. I walked a long way, still carrying my parachute, maps and Sidcot. It was bloody hot. Eventually I walked into a small French town, found the town hall and an official, from whom I begged a car to take me to Calais.

We drove past miles and miles of civilians in carts, bicycles, lorries, prams, old folk, young folk, kids and hundreds of French soldiers, all heading west. What a terrible and depressing shambles. We made Calais and I went aboard, and by 10 pm that evening was back in the Officers' Mess at RAF Station Hawkinge. Next day I found myself in Folkestone Hospital where they put me to sleep and fixed my nose. Three weeks later I was able to re-join 605, which was back in Scotland.

Lance Sergeant Charlie Constantine (3rd Grenadier Guards):-

We were all occupied firing at different movements and targets. Our Bren gunner was standing up and firing through a hole in the wall to my left when suddenly he screamed in agony, his weapon falling to the floor – he had been hit in the eye and was in a terrible state. I got to him quickly and held him to see what could be done. I tried to get his hands away from his eye to inspect the damage but he broke away from me screaming in agony. He ran to the end of the barn where two of the Section tried to hold him, but again he broke free. Before we could stop him he ran out of the door, out of his mind. By now, things outside had got worse. Light mortar bombs were now falling on our position and I knew that once they had ranged in on the barn we wouldn't stand a chance.

A German soldier had got into some cover about 25 yards away, whilst I had been away from my position. Suddenly he got up and ran towards the barn, raising an automatic weapon, preparing to fire. I fired first and saw him fall. I then fired another shot at the body on the ground, just in case, and put some rounds slightly to the right where I sensed other movement.

Things quietened down during the afternoon, and it started raining heavily. We remained in our positions and by nightfall word reached us that our Battalion's line had held once more. Not long afterwards we received orders to withdraw, and learned that the Battalion had suffered many casualties.

Flight Lieutenant Gerry Edge:-

The roads below were full of columns of civilians and soldiers, all progressing westwards. Once we came upon a Ju 87 Stuka that was strafing a column of refugees. It was plain to anyone, especially from that height, that this was a civilian, as opposed to a military, column. I am pleased to say that I shot this Boche down. There were no survivors. Does that concern me? Not at all. Of all the enemy aircraft I shot down, that one gave me great pleasure.

Flight Lieutenant Gerry Edge (right), at Hawkinge during the Battle of Britain.

Squadron Leader Teddy Donaldson DSO:-

The Low Countries refused to allow British troops in before the Germans broke through. Then the French bolted, including their air force. I have never seen so many people running so fast anywhere, so long as it was west. The poor British soldiers were continuously let down when Dutch, Belgian and French soldiers surrendered by the division. The British were marvellous and finally fought their way to the flat beaches of Dunkirk.

151 Squadron at North Weald, 1940. Squadron Leader Teddy Donaldson at third left (talking to the Station Commander, Group Captain Victor Beamish), and Pilot Officer Jack Hamar at fourth right.

Lieutenant Peter Halliday (2nd Hampshires):-

A Section of a Lancashire regiment stumbled past, which had evidently been reduced to a very tired looking Corporal and an even wearier looking private soldier. The private stopped and sat down by the roadside. I have found a certain four-letter word to be grammatically flexible, and this was now demonstrated. "Corporal", said the private, "Ah'm fooked". The Corporal was obviously at the end of his tether and threw his rifle to the ground. "Fooked be fooked!", he cried, "All the fookers is fooked, you stupid fooker!"

Squadron Leader Teddy Donaldson DSO:-

The aerial fighting was not altogether difficult, however, as the Germans were grossly over confident. The trouble was, we had to go back to Manston at night because we had damaged aircraft but no ground crews with us in France to repair them. Next day we were back to France, and this continued daily because our airfields in France were being heavily bombed. Whilst pilots could get away and sleep off the airfield, the Hurricanes would have taken a terrific beating on the ground. 151 Squadron flew as many as seven sorties a day against overwhelming odds.

Pilot Officer Jack Hamar DFC:-

The leader ordered Red Section to attack and we dived towards the Ju 87s. I lost sight of the leader and circled to select a target. I closed on one which was diving, but failed to attack before the E/A dropped its bombs on a village. As the E/A pulled up I attacked, giving a five second burst at 200 yards which killed the rear gunner. I closed to 100 yards and after a seven second burst the E/A turned on its side with smoke pouring from its engine. It went into a steep dive and crashed in a field. I then attacked another E/A at which I fired a short burst from 200 yards, after which I experienced no further fire from the rear. I closed to 100 yards and opened fire, which tore off the side of the fuselage and top of port wing. I was forced to break away without observing what happened to this E/A because I ran into another five Ju 87s. I did not see any further E/A crash but I saw a parachute descending. Having turned the petrol supply onto the gravity tank, and having just 15 rounds per gun remaining, I returned to base.

Squadron Leader Teddy Donaldson DSO:-

At Dunkirk we even stayed on patrol after running out of ammunition to complete a one-hour patrol. This hindered the *Luftwaffe* from attacking the defenceless troops on the ground. When we finally returned to North Weald, we were involved in escorting RAF bombers attacking German communications and the thousands of invasion barges massing along the Pas de Calais beaches, rivers and canals. Most, if not all, of the Hurricane squadrons which had operated from French airfields had by this time been rested, except 151. Basil Embry, a man without fear, was commanding a bomber squadron in those days, and always asked for 151 as escort because we always stayed close.

One of the pilots we lost was Allen Ives. He was partially trained to be a doctor, so I gave my permission for him to remain on the beaches to help treat badly wounded soldiers. He put up a marvellous show before getting on a boat. This was sunk and 'Ivy' was swimming in the sea when shot through the head by a German soldier who was lying on the bow deck of an 'E'-boat. An eyewitness account of the incident was given to me by another 151 Squadron pilot, a New Zealander, also shot down over Dunkirk.

Squadron Leader 'Tubby' Mermagen:-

By June 3rd, the wretched evacuation appeared complete – no life could be seen either on the beaches or on the country behind. During Operation DYNAMO I lost four pilots killed and another 'missing', all whilst flying from RAF Hornchurch.

Air Commodore HW 'Tubby' Mermagen pictured in Germany, 1945.

Flight Lieutenant Brian Lane DFC:-

Yes, the show was over now. The enemy was within 20 miles of our coast, but another show would be put on, many shows perhaps, and Hitler would *never* speak the last line.

Pilot Officer David Scott-Malden:-

I remember very clearly that whilst training to fly Spitfires at Aston Down, during June 1940, we treated flying under the Severn Bridge rather as a parting gesture when we were already safely posted to a squadron and reasonably safe from any complaints to the authorities. There are several large arches in the railway-bridge, and two smaller ones on the Welsh side. I had long arguments with my friend George Barclay about whether a Spitfire could get through one of the smaller arches. He decided that it could get through on the diagonal, i.e. with the wings at 45° to the horizontal. We watched whilst he demonstrated his theory in practice, and were somewhat relieved when George emerged safely the other side! Personally I played safe and used one of the larger arches, although such flights will not be found recorded in any pilots' logbooks – not if they were wise!

Whilst at Aston Down I recorded the following diary entries:-

Monday 10th June: War declared on the British and French by Mussolini. We now face the prospect of fighting in North Africa and the Mediterranean.

Wednesday 12th June: Had a test on a Harvard and passed successfully into Spitfire flight. First solo an indescribable thrill. Felt a pretty king man!

Friday 14th June: Paris falls. Astonishing to think of it in the hands of the Germans. Reynaud declares "Will fight on even if driven out of France". Marvellous days doing aerobatics in Spitfires.

Monday 17th June: The French give up hostilities. Cannot yet conceive the enormity of it all. I suppose it will not be long before we are defending England in earnest.

Thursday 20th June: Reports of another raid in South Wales. Fired eight Brownings into the River Severn for the first time. This getting up at 4.30 a.m. is beginning to tell.

Air Vice-Marshal David Scott-Malden (now deceased), receives from the author a mounted artefact of Spitfire R6644, which he flew in 1940.

(Mark Postelthwaite)

Winston Churchill:-

Even though large tracts of Europe and many old and famous States have fallen, or may fall into the grip of the Gestapo and all the odious apparatus of Nazi rule, we shall not flag or fail. We shall go on to the end.... We shall fight on the seas and oceans, we shall fight with growing confidence and growing strength in the air. We shall fight on the beaches, we shall fight on the landing grounds, we shall fight in the fields and in the streets, we shall fight in the hills, we shall never surrender.

Adolf Hitler:-

As England, in spite of her hopeless military position, has so far shown herself unwilling to come to any compromise, I have decided to begin preparations for, and if necessary, cary out the invasion of England.

The operation is dictated by the necessity to eliminate Great Britain as a base from which the war against Germany can be fought. If necessary the island will be occupied. I therefore issue the following orders:-

1. The landing operation must be a surprise crossing on a broad front extending approximately from Ramsgate to a point west of the Isle of Wight. The preparations must be concluded by the middle of August.

2. The following preparations must be undertaken to make a landing in England possible:-

    a)   The English air force must be eliminated to such an extent that it will be incapable of putting up any substantial opposition to the invading troops...

Winston Churchill:-

What General Weygand called the Battle of France is over. I expect that the Battle of Britain is about to begin. Upon this battle depends the survival of Christian civilisation... The whole fury and might of the enemy must very soon be turned upon us. Hitler knows that he will have to break us in this island or lose the war. If we can stand up to him, all Europe may be free and the life of the world may move forward into broad, sunlit uplands. But if we fail, then the whole world, including the United States, including all that we have known and cared for, will sink into the abyss of a new Dark Age made more sinister, and perhaps more protracted, by the lights of perverted science. Let us therefore brace ourselves to our duties, and so bear ourselves that if the British Empire and its Commonwealth lasts for a thousand years, men will still say "This was their finest hour".

Chapter Eighteen

Vignettes: 2

Squadron Leader Harry Hogan DFC:-

Some of our Hurricane squadron's replacement pilots were straight from OTU, and these we tried to get into the air as soon as possible to provide a little extra experience. We were just too tired, though, to give any dogfighting practice at all. They were all very green, youngsters who were completely bewildered and lost in action.

Pilot Officer Peter Olver:-

At the time I was strongly under the impression that the war would be over before I could get into it, so I applied for a posting to a fighter squadron in the south of England immediately after OTU. Fortunately for me, however, on September 30th I was sent to 611 Squadron at Digby, in 12 Group, with which I remained for 16 days and logged a further 18 hours on Spitfires, some of it operational. Then my posting came to 603 Squadron at Hornchurch, but I was shot down by an Me 109 on my first trip, October 25th, 1940.

Squadron Leader George Denholm DFC:-

After an action the Squadron never returned to Hornchurch as a cohesive unit, but in ones and twos.

Pilot Officer George Pushman:-

We of 23 Squadron were based at Wittering, but flew mostly from Ford during the Battle of Britain which was a very busy period. We used to have 10 days on duty followed by two days off. Flying at night in our Blenheims, we prowled around the east-coast, but I never caught even a glimpse of a German aircraft.

George Pushman, a Canadian, whilst serving as a Flight Lieutenant at the time of D-Day and flying Bostons. Sadly he died in 2001.

Squadron Leader Teddy Donaldson DSO:-

Jack Hamar was my Number Two on that fateful day, July 24th, 1940. A leader has to navigate as well as co-ordinate and lead attacks. He can only do this if he has a good Number Two, whom he could completely rely on. A CO then knows that no one can creep up behind him so long as his Number Two is in place. I always knew that Jack would be there. If he were shot down, I knew that the last thing he would do would be to tell me on the radio that he had 'had it'. Looking after me was an extremely hazardous task. Jack did it loyally and even so managed to shoot down six-and-a-half enemy aircraft. The 'half' was for a German bomber that we shared; I had damaged it but it may have returned to base, so Jack blew it out of the sky in flames. During the war, I made nine forced landings in total, but I was never shot down with Jack Hamar as my Number Two.

Jack and I were extremely close, I loved the fellow. From mid-July we slept the night in dugouts at North Weald. There were eight pilots on camp beds at the beginning. By July 24th, only Jack and I were left. On the previous night Jack had sat on my bed and said "Sir, I think you and I will live through all this. We have been to hell and back together but are still alive".

I said "For God's sake don't say that, its bad luck".

The next morning the weather was appalling. I got an urgent telephone call from the Air Officer Commanding (Air Vice-Marshal Park). He said "The weather is awful but I have an unidentified aircraft circling Felixstowe at 10,000 feet and I don't like it. As the weather is so bad, I must ask, not order, you: can you go after him?"

I said to Jack "What about it?"

He said, as I knew he would, "Let's get the bastard!"

Air Vice-Marshal Park said "Thanks a lot", so off we went. Visibility was down to about a quarter of a mile. The danger at North Weald was the international radar masts. These went up to several hundred feet, and whilst the Controllers could get pilots back to the airfield, to avoid the masts you had to see them in time.

No sooner than we were airborne with wheels up than Group identified the aircraft circling Felixstowe as friendly. We turned around and, flying slowly at 120 mph and some 60 feet above the ground, I waited for North Weald to re-appear, which it did in a few minutes. I signalled to Jack to 'break'. To my horror he broke upwards and commenced an upward roll. It was impossible to carry out such a manoeuvre in a Hurricane at that low speed. As I saw him start his right-handed roll, I screamed "Don't! Don't!" down the R/T, but it was too late. Jack stalled and hit the ground upside down.

I was on the ground and beside him within seconds. Jack had his hood open to improve visibility in the awful weather conditions, and this had caused massive head injuries.

I was devastated.

Pilot Officer Wallace Cunningham DFC:-

We of 19 Squadron were lying in the sun at Coltishall along with Douglas Bader and other 222 Squadron pilots. It was just before our involvement in the Battle of Britain proper and our Brian Lane had received a 'gong' for his good leadership of the Squadron and general activities at Dunkirk. Douglas was kidding him and asked Brian "What's that?" in his usual cocky fashion, pointing to Brian's DFC ribbon.

"Hmm. I must get one of those", said Bader, and, as we all know, he did.

Flight Lieutenant Wallace 'Jock' Cunningham DFC receives a model of Spitfire P9546, in which he destroyed an Me 109 during the Battle of Britain, at a Ramrod launch, 1995. The base includes artefacts from this particular Spitfire, the remains of which were recovered by the author and friends in 1993.

(Andrew Long)

Air Vice-Marshal Keith Park:-

The main problem was to know which was the diversionary attack and to hold sufficient fighter squadrons in readiness to meet the main attack when this could be discerned from the very unreliable information received from the RDF, after they had been heavily bombed. To meet these attacks on coastal objectives, it was essential to keep nearly all Readiness squadrons at forward aerodromes, such as Lympne, Hawkinge, Manston, Rochford. The greatest vigilance had to be observed by Group Controller not to have these squadrons bombed or machine-gunned on the ground at forward aerodromes. On only one occasion was any squadron at a forward aerodrome attacked while on the ground refuelling, and this was because the squadron failed to maintain a protective patrol over the base during refuelling.

A very high state of preparedness has to be maintained in order to engage the enemy before he reached his coastal objectives. The general plan in employing the fighters was to detail about half the available squadrons, including the Spitfires, to engage the enemy fighters, and the remainder to attack the enemy bombers, which normally flew at between 11,000 and 13,000 feet, and carried out their attack frequently from 7,000 to 8,000 feet.

During this phase our fighters were mainly employing the Fighter Command attacks from astern. These gave good results against the enemy fighters, which were unarmoured, but were not so effective against the bombers. Our fighters were therefore advised to practise deflection shots from quarter astern, also from above and from below against twin-engined bombers.

During this phase, fighter squadrons not infrequently flew over fifty hours in one day with twelve aircraft in commission.

The casualties to pilots and aircraft were about equal in numbers for any given engagement. Owing to the lack of trained formation and section leaders, also to the fitting of armour to enemy bombers, our casualties were relatively higher than during May and June, when operating over France and Belgium.

Results (of air combat) were satisfactory, the proportion of enemy shot down to our own losses being about four to one, slightly below the average when fighting over France. As much of this fighting took place over the sea, casualties were higher than they would have been if the fighting had been over land. The results of air combat were good because the enemy fighters were frequently too high to protect their bombers. Moreover, the Ju 87 proved an easy prey to both Hurricanes and Spitfires.

Group Captain AB 'Woody' Woodhall:-

Most of the Czech pilots reported in French uniform. On arrival in England they spoke little English, and had to be converted on to Hurricanes. They were therefore provided with with an English squadron commander, Squadron Leader Douglas Blackwood, and English flight commanders, Flight Lieutenants Sinclair and Jeffries, in addition to both an English flying instructor and interpreter.

The Czech CO was Squadron Leader Sacha Hess who was quite famous in Czech Air Force circles. Much older than the rest, at 45, he was a first class pilot and a dedicated fighter. His English counterpart was Squadron Leader Blackwood, who also had two English flight

Group Captain 'Woody' Woodhall 'in the mood'!

commanders, Sinclair and Jeffries.

Our first problem was to overcome the language difficulty, so I rang the BBC with the result that the interpreter and I spent a day at Broadcasting House where we recorded a series of orders, first in English followed by Czech, covering every order from 'Scramble' to 'Pancake'. The BBC quickly sent us several copies of these records, and in a very short time the Czechs were conversant with orders in English alone.

310 Squadron had a spare Hurricane (needless to say it was the oldest and slowest) which was always at my disposal, and as a result, on the few occasions when I could spare the time from my other duties as Station Commander and Sector Controller, I flew on operations with this squadron as rear-end Charlie.

Squadron Leader Douglas Blackwood:-

I cannot speak highly enough of the Czechs' fighting qualities, although I must admit that they did not always do what was expected of them; they were very keen on attacking enemy aircraft whenever they saw them, no matter what the circumstances. At first we had a great deal of difficulty with the lack of a common language as only a few of them understood even basic English. We overcame this difficulty by various means, however.

Flight Lieutenant Gordon Sinclair DFC:-

I have nothing but praise for my fellow Czech pilots. They were a wonderful bunch of people totally determined to kill Germans. They went about this task with great enthusiasm and courage. I personally found it tremendously comforting in battle to have such pilots around me!

LAC Bill Kirk (Orderly Clerk, 310 Squadron):-

The Czechs were first class and were anxious to have a go, but it was some time before they were considered to be operationally equal to the other squadrons because they just hadn't had the RAF's training. Once they got into the swim though I think they did very well. It became a tradition for us all to have a Czech top button on our RAF tunics. I was amongst the party sent to form 310 Squadron, at which time I was a Corporal. In the Orderly Room we did everything, all the admin from combat reports to leave passes and Air Ministry Orders. Even now I remember that the Form 1623 was airframes and engines! Working hours were non-existent, you just went on until the job was finished. I lived in the barrack block at Duxford and we got on very well with the Czechs. They were always keeping fit, playing volley ball, and were very keen generally. For us on the ground it was tremendously exciting knowing that the aircraft were going into action, and when they returned we all looked anxiously for those with blown gunport patches, indicating that the guns had been fired. It could also be distressing, talking to a chap in the Mess one night only for him to be a 'gonner' the next day. My office was almost on the airfield itself, so we were very close to the pilots and aircraft. I never heard anyone complain about not being in the action, however, so far as I was aware we were being used as much as was either possible or appropriate. I also recall that 'Woody' Woodhall was a bit of a character!

Pilot Officer 'Teddy' Morten:-

I received my commission in late June 1940, and was posted to RAF Duxford for supernumerary duties in 'Operations'; the 'VR' letters on my lapel shone brightly on my tunic. There were several of us who arrived at the same time, including an elderly Pilot Officer who was a retired solicitor. We were all introduced to the Station Commander, Wing Commander AB Woodhall. The old solicitor was wearing a Boer

War ribbon on his tunic, but 'Woody' asked him where his 1914-18 ribbons were; 'I was too old for the Great War', he replied, and so the Wing Commander decided that, due to his general experience of life, he should become assistant adjutant to 19 Squadron, to help the CO write his casualty letters.

At that time, the Sector Controllers were, first and foremost, Wing Commander Woodhall, Squadron Leader

KC Horn, who had commanded a squadron of Strutters (his brother was a successful Sopwith Camel commander), Squadron Leader Marsden, Squadron Leader Stanley Cooper, and Squadron Leader Livivosk.

As dawn broke each day that summer, if on duty at Ops 'B', the Controller would be resting (i.e. asleep only to be disturbed if necessary). Straight after dawn, I would telephone Wing Commander Woodhall on his direct line and inform him of the situation over southern England. There was dire trouble if ever 'Woody' was not told first!

As an embryonic Controller, a 'Wingless Wonder' or 'Penguin', I always made it my business to get to know as many pilots as possible, so as to gain their trust and understand the problems they faced in the air. All of us on the ground, of course, wanted to help them as much as possible.

Group Captain 'Woody' Woodhall:-

When I first arrived at Duxford, it was as 'Squadron Leader Flying Ops.' and second in command to Wing Commander 'Pingo' Lester. In addition to being administrative officer I was made responsible for the development of the Fighter Control System and the training of operations room crews. It was at Sector level that fighter control became a personal affair. From the Sector Station the Controller was in direct communication with the fighter pilots by R/T. With the introduction of VHF R/T, the distances at which one could communicate was increased tremendously.

When I arrived at Duxford there was only a skeleton operations room crew. The priority was to train sufficient personnel to man the operations room on a 24 hour basis. When the WAAF came into being, we were delighted to get female plotters. These girls were a credit to the Air Force, and were so good looking that an officer from Group HQ christened them as 'Woody's Beauty Chorus'!

Jill 'Half Pint' Pepper (a WAAF plotter in 'Woody's Beauty Chorus'):-

Jill 'Half Pint' Pepper pictured in the restored Ops Room at the IWM Duxord, 1995. During the Battle of Britain, Jill, now Mrs Nielsen and living in Norway, was 19-years old.

In 1939 and part of 1940, the Duxford Operations Room was situated on the station. Later it was moved some way outside and rebuilt in a sort of shed in a copse. A bus took us there to go on watch. The Operations Room has since been reconstructed at the IWM Duxford Airfield and is very authentic.

In 12 Group we did not get much action. The atmosphere was quiet and we had plenty of time to chat with the Observer Corps on the other end of our headphones. Voices can be very misleading and we sometimes got quite a shock when we met the blokes in person!

After Dunkirk things got more lively and we were kept busy on our watches - concentration and calmness were essential to get the plotting right. The planes went up and it was always exciting when we heard 'Tally Ho!' over the intercom. We felt then that we were doing our bit to help stop the 'bloody Huns'. It was sad, though, when some of our aircraft failed to return, even if we did not know the pilots personally.

There were often dances too in the big hangar and whenever I hear 'In the Mood' I'm back there again and can see the Station Commander, Wing Commander Woodhall, complete with monocle, playing his clarinet with great enthusiasm!

Sergeant Reg Johnson:-

When I became the first VR pilot to join 222 Squadron, a regular unit, in April 1940, I found that the Squadron was addicted to tight formation flying, for which I had no training whatsoever. A study of the pre-war flying career of our CO, Squadron Leader Mermagen, might however explain this addiction, particularly in respect of making us fly so tight that our wings actually overlapped. In three behind three we even looped in formation! We even rolled as a squadron on one occasion! Mermagen was himself an exceptional pilot, but such training proved unsuitable for the Battle of Britain that lay ahead, although at the time he did not enjoy the benefits of hindsight.

When 222 went south to Hornchurch, we lost eight Spitfires and a number of pilots in the first 48 hours. We had gone into action flying our tight formation, as a result of which our losses were heavy. Eventually we evolved a weaving 'Tail-end Charlie' section, which weaved about above, below and to the rear of our formation. Although this helped a little it was still not the complete answer. As a permanent member of Green Section, I was given the weaving job along with Pilot Officer Laurie Whitbread and one other.

Pilot Officer 'Teddy' Morten:-

The 11 Group Controllers definitely called for 12 Group too late. By the end of August there was a certain amount of hostility between the respective Operations Rooms. 11 Group accused us of always being too late, we said that they called for us too late. Whenever 12 Group squadrons arrived after the action, we would have to suffer sarcastic remarks from the 11 Group Controller, so the situation was not good.

Group Captain Woodhall:-

In those early days, the RDF information was not very accurate, particularly regarding height and numbers of aircraft, and of course there was a time lag of several minutes before the information reached the Sector Operations Room. The Sector Controller therefore had to use intelligent guesswork to direct his fighters on an intercepting course and also to position them up-sun, above the enemy. To begin with, the operations table in No 12 Group only extended to the North bank of the Thames, and enemy plots were only passed to us when they reached this point. In No 11 Group however, enemy plots were received whilst the enemy was still over France. Command Operations Room had the whole picture, of course, but in my opinion there was never enough liaison between 11 and 12 Groups.

Luckily, Wing Commander Victor Beamish, the Sector Commander at North Weald, was a good friend of mine, so I extended our operations table to the south as far into France as St Omer, and as soon as North Weald were informed of enemy activity, we kept the tie-line telephone open, and the plots were passed from North Weald to Duxford. In that way we obtained earlier warning, but in spite of this, we were frequently scrambled too late because we were not allowed to fly over 11 Group territory unless asked for by them. It was frustrating to see an enemy raid plotted on our board, obviously going for a target in 11 Group, then to wait on the ground, with the pilots in their cockpits for 15 or 20 minutes, and finally to be scrambled too late to get into the fight.

Flying Officer Frank Brinsden:-

During late August 1940, I always felt a bit cheated as we of 19 Squadron always seemed to be late off the ground and therefore too late to intercept; we often arrived over the battle zone only to find that all had gone home.

Flying Officer Frank Brinsden at Fowlmere. Captured whilst brought down flying Mosquitoes on the famous Peenemunde Raid in 1944, Frank, a New Zealander living in Australia, visited the author in 1990, but sadly died soon afterwards.

Squadron Leader Gerry Edge DFC:-

They didn't like that head-on attack, you know, but you had to judge the break-away point right. If you left it to the last 100 yards then you were in trouble, due to the fast closing speeds, but once you got the hang of it a head-on attack was a piece of cake. When you opened fire, you'd kill or badly wound the pilot and second pilot. Then you'd rake the whole line as you broke away. On one attack the first *Heinkel* I hit crashed into the next.

Flying Officer James Coward:-

Flight Lieutenant Clouston led us into a copybook Fighter Command No 1 Attack from dead ahead, turning in three sections line astern, to come up in sections echelon port behind the enemy who were in sections of three in vic line astern. Our fourth section, led by Flying Officer Frank Brinsden, was detailed to climb and intercept the fighters. I got a cannon shell through the cockpit which shattered my left leg below

Air Commodore James Coward pictured whilst recently visiting England from his home in Australia.

the knee, also severing the elevator controls, and I had to bale out. I put a tourniquet around my thigh, using my helmet radio lead, and landed by parachute about four miles north of Duxford on the Royston to Newmarket Road. I was admitted to Addenbroke's Hospital in Cambridge and was obviously out of the battle from then on.

Group Captain Woodhall:-

On the first occasion the Czechs got into action, early in the Battle of Britain, they made an excellent showing. I met them on their return to the aerodrome and spoke with Sacha Hess; he had disabled a Dornier over Epping Forest which made a wheels-up forced-landing in a field. He followed it down with the intention of making certain that no-one got out of it alive. He saw three Germans climb out, who, when they realised that Sacha was diving on them, held up their hands. To quote his own words: 'I hesitate, then it was too late, so I go round again to make sure I kill them - they wave something white - again I do not shoot - then (disgustedly) I think it is no use, I am become too bloody British!'

Hess had good cause to hate the Germans; he had recently received notification that both his wife and daughter had been killed by the Nazis.

Squadron Leader Douglas Blackwood:-

The Big Wing thing was all started by Douglas Bader, who of course had a Cranwell background, and so he naturally became leader. At the time, I was younger than he, and had received command of 310 Squadron shortly after Douglas received 242. Certainly amongst the three squadrons initially involved, Douglas was the senior squadron commander; Brian Lane had only just received command of 19 Squadron so although he had the most combat experience, he was the most junior Squadron Leader in the Sector. When Douglas suggested the Wing, as he was senior, we just automatically assumed that he would lead. He was a *very* forceful character, of course, and so even if we had wanted to, it would have been impossible to argue with him! An example of this occurred when we were together at Duxford during the making of the 'Battle of Britain' film; Douglas was there as a consultant but would not stop interfering with the shoot. In the end the Director said 'I'm making this film, not you' and ordered him off the set. That was Douglas to a 'T'. In 1940, his ideas regarding the Big Wing had the support of the Duxford Station Commander, Wing Commander Woodhall, but even he could not have stood up to Douglas if it had ever come to that, he just said 'I'm doing this', and that was that. There is no doubt, however, that Douglas Bader was a very brave man and it was because of the way he conquered his disabilities caused by the crash in 1931, that he became popular amongst his acquaintances - his 242 Squadron pilots would have followed him anywhere. We are talking, after all, about a man who played squash well and had a low golf handicap despite having no legs!

I think that we should have been requested earlier as that would have enabled us to climb out to sea and then attack high over the Thames Estuary. But I think that *everyone* was doing their best, we were all learning. 11 Group felt that it was their responsibility to defend London without 12 took-off, heading for Debden and North Weald.

Pilot Officer Roger Hall:-

We saw our own fighters - the 11 Group squadrons, and some from 12 Group in the Midlands - climbing up from the north. There seemed to be quite a number of us. They too were black dots, climbing in groups of 12 or 36 in Wing formation. Most of them were Hurricanes.

I recalled for an instant Mr Baldwin's prophecy, not a sanguine one, made to the House of Commons some five years before when he said that the bomber would always get through. Now it was doing just that.

Squadron Leader Harry Fenton:-

Our routine was to rise before first light, about 0330 hrs, have a coffee and then go to dispersal. We then spent the day there, being scrambled at intervals in either squadron or section strength. we shared Middle Wallop with 609 Squadron and so took it in turns to spend every third day down at Warmwell undertaking convoy protection patrols. That was during the early days, but I was shot down and wounded on August 8th, returning to the squadron on September 12th. By that time 238 had been back at Middle Wallop for two days but we already had two pilots missing from action over 11 Group: David Hughes, an able flight commander, and a Polish pilot, Duszinski, whom I had not met. As you rightly say, the tempo of combat had totally changed.

Sergeant Gordon Batt:-

When we returned to Middle Wallop in September, the size of German formations had increased: the bomber formations were usually 50-60 strong, in an oblong block and in close formation, and above then were Me 110s, and Me 109s higher still. To counter this, we often flew together with one of Wallop's Spitfire squadrons. Our CO was the senior squadron commander and so we usually led, our

Hurricanes attacking the bombers whilst the Spitfires held off the escort. It certainly did my morale a hell of a lot of good, God and Hitler knew what it did to theirs! The only snag was that as 238 were first to attack, I never had the opportunity to look back - there must have been chaos! Towards the end of August and throughout September, we were frequently called to the west of London area. The Controller would give us a commentary regarding what was going on generally, and, whilst we held off at 20,000', could hear him directing 11 Group squadrons into action. From our position west of London, we could see the ack-ack bursting over the capital, and condensation trails of the Spitfires, Hurricanes and Me 109s; the boys of 11 Group were obviously holding their own and we were sensibly being held in reserve. When we were vectored, the Controller would say something like: '25 Bandits Angels 20, heading straight for you, they're all yours!' It really was slick control.

Pilot Officer Arthur Vokes:-

'B' Flight attacked 6 Do 17s, one breaking away chased by F/Sgt Steere and self. One Jerry baled out. One Me 110 surprised me and bored a hole in starboard wing. After two or three turns I got on his tail and gave him everything. Dived vertically into cloud, starboard engine smoking. One probable Me 110. Hundreds of Jerries!

Sergeant Reg Johnson:-

My recollection is that the engagement during which Pilot Officer Laurie Whitbread was lost was a 'B' Flight commitment only, led by Pilot Officer Broadhurst in Blue Section, followed by Pilot Officer Whitbread, myself and another in Green. We climbed to the suicidal height of 14,000 feet and stooged around in tight formation with only one pair of eyes available to scan the sky in front, over perhaps 200°. We didn't deserve to be jumped, but we certainly invited it. We were banking gently to the left, which allowed me at No 3 to look over the top of No 1, and I shouted the warning "Bandits, 2 'o' clock above, attacking!" I turned over and dived.

There is no way that Pilot Officer Whitbread could even have seen the enemy, formating as he was on the aircraft to his left and with three quarters of his head and back to our attackers. When I left it was his right side facing the 109s, which were already in firing range. I can only assume that having received my warning he too rolled to the right, exposing his left side to the enemy and was hit before he could commence his dive. It was a tragedy.

Pilot Officer John Greenwood:-

I remember being with Sergeant Kee and diving for our lives into cloud. As I recall he copped a little enemy fire and we landed together shortly afterwards having made no effort to locate the rest of the Squadron. Kee's aircraft had a little fabric missing and a few holes. I stopped an armour-piercing bullet through my head armour, the core of which bullet lodged in my neck. It had only just penetrated and was as sharp as a needle. I kept it as a souvenir for many years.

Pilot Officer Geoff Wellum:-

During September and October, there were always 109s in numbers over our Sector at Biggin Hill. They were always above us as we were always scrambled too late to achieve sufficient height. Our climb was always a desperate, full throttle affair but we never seemed to quite get up to them. On one patrol I did manage to get a crack at two 109s, but although I saw strikes could only claim them as damaged.

Sergeant 'Taffy' Higginson:-

Sergeant 'Taffy' Higginson DFM at 'Readiness'.

I remember thinking that morale might be better if we had a Squadron Mascot, so I went into the local town and bought a small monkey which we named '109'. He was a great success and was kept in a cage and on a lead. Anyway, the Station Commander gave a cocktail party for our 56 Squadron and suggested that 109 should be present. He was, and went down very well, until, that is, he started to undertake enthusiastic sexual self-gratification! Morals being what they were in those days, we had to remove 109 very quickly!

Sergeant Tony Pickering:-

Tony Pickering, the first of the Few that the author actually met, proudly displays his bound flying log-books, 1988.

I was 18 during the Battle of Britain and came from a small village where everyone knew everyone else. We went to school, did our homework in the evenings, and went to church on Sundays. We were innocents, really, the RAF was a bit of a culture shock, all these chaps who were going around night clubs and girls! It was something to touch a girl's arm at a dance in those days, don't forget, not like it is now!

Sergeant Norman Ramsay:-

People missing or killed at that stage of the battle meant little to me. I had joined 222 from 610 at Biggin Hill after we had lost 10, yes 10, pilots, so I was well used to the disappearing faces. Having been shot down myself I had learned to survive, to get the experience necessary for survival.

Sergeant Bernard 'Jimmy' Jennings DFM:-

Casualties? Well, when it came to that sort of thing we just didn't talk about it much, didn't dwell upon that sort of thing. It was just a case of 'Old so and so's copped it', and that was it.

Sergeant Bernard 'Jimmy' Jennings DFM.

Chapter Nineteen

Postscript

Astute readers may have noticed that many of the preceding accounts concern personnel from 10 and 12 Groups, rather than just, or in the main, 11 Group. In this, and in addition to exposing the contribution made by the 'also rans' in general and VR pilots in particular, and not having forgotten the support staff, my intention was to offer a slightly different slant on the generally published format of such books. The Battle of Britain was really just that. It really was the Battle of *Britain*, and was not *exclusively* fought over London and the Southeast. Many, I suspect, do not fully appreciate just how much fighting took place over the West Country and the South Coast, particularly from Portland east to Portsmouth.

One thing that I hope has come through clearly is my personal love for the subject and, indeed, the friends featured in this book. The downside to that has been that in recent years I have lost an increasing number of them: as time marches on so the Few get fewer. Battle of Britain pilot Brian Kingcombe once wrote that whenever he visits his former wartime station he feels that he 'walks with ghosts'. That I can understand. Sat here writing this in my office, in which are stored not only the personal effects of certain casualties that have been passed on to me over the years but also *reams* of my correspondence with the Few, many of whom are now deceased, I feel surrounded by ghosts.

The Battle of Britain ranks amongst the most decisive battles in world history, and not surprisingly the survivors, who also came through four more years of war, remember those days with mixed emotions. For all, however, they remain memories of what was probably the most exciting time of their lives, albeit years punctuated by fear and sadness, and conversely purpose and exhilaration. Many of these men were only able to achieve their true potential or destiny as a result of opportunities provided by the outbreak of war. Would all of those who became pilots through the RAF VR have become fighter pilots if not for the war, for example? I think not, flying would have remained the preserve of Cranwellians and Short Service Commissioned officers of the regular service. For many, therefore, the war was a unique opportunity to learn about oneself, to know one's limits in all respects, to experience many things, good and bad, which would have been impossible in peacetime.

Fortunately historians dealing with the wartime years have enjoyed advantages provided by our computerised age. We have been able to record the experiences of survivors in a way that was not possible for the veterans of, say, Hastings, Waterloo or Trafalgar. That having been said, I wish that when I started this project so many years ago, the benefits of the world-wide-web and digital recording equipment had been available! Reference material is also much more detailed, comprehensive and widely available today, than say 20 years ago, which makes research very much easier. Again though we come back full circle to the crux of the matter: our heroes, our greatest primary source, are leaving us, one by one.

The other thing we at Ramrod have done is literally bring the Battle of Britain to the High Street, through our book launches at Worcester Guildhall, and give the general public an opportunity to meet and personally thank the veterans. Moreover, from a personal perspective, it gives me great satisfaction to know that Flying Officer Franek Surma now has a personal memorial, and that the graves of two pilots merely recorded as 'unknown' have been officially accepted and identified as being those Flying Officer Cutts and Sergeant Brimble. That though, as they say, is another story.

The photographs in this section show some of the gatherings at a small number of our Ramrod book launches and other events since foundation of this operation in 1992. What a rich tapestry of memories these occasions have become, and what a privilege. It is unlikely that there will be many more, for obvious reasons, but when we gather with our heroes over the next couple of years, I hope to see you there!

Boys toys: the author, aged nine, on the first occasion that he actually saw a Spitfire! This, and the 1969 Battle of Britain film he describes as 'immeasurably inspiring and planted the seed of what has now become'.

At the launch of The Invisible Thread *and the Surma Memorial Trust for Youth, the registered charity founded by the artist Mark Postlethwaite and the author, Great Malvern, 1992. From left to right: Group Captain Gerry Edge, Wing Commander 'Jimmy' Jennings, Mr Fred Roberts, Hans 'Peter' Wulff, Squadron Leader Harry Welford, Flight Lieutenant William Walker, Flight Lieutenant Ken Wilkinson, Flying Officer John Lumsden, Squadron Leader 'Buck' Casson, Flight Lieutenant Richard Jones, Flight Lieutenant Peter Taylor, Warrant Officer 'Butch' Morton, Flight Lieutenants Peter Hairs, Hugh Chalmers, Tadek Turek, Kzek Budzik & Tadek Dzidzic. Of those pictured, six are sadly now deceased.*

Back at Great Malvern in 1993 for the launch of Through Peril to the Stars. From left to right: Wing Commander 'Jimmy' Jennings, Squadron Leaders 'Steve' Stevens and Bob Pugh, Flight Lieutenant Tony Minchin, Squadron Leader 'Buck' Casson, Wing Commander George 'Grumpy' Unwin, Flight Lieutenants Ken Wilkinson, Tadek Dzidzic, Denis Nichols, Ron Rayner and Duncan Spruce, Squadron Leader Iain Hutchinson, Flight Lieutenants William Walker and Richard Jones, and Group Captain Gerry Edge. Sadly, three of those pictured have since died.

The author at yet another book launch, this time honoured by the presence of Air Chief Marshal Sir Christopher Foxley-Norris and the composer Ron Goodwin, whose film scores include not only Battle of Britain but also 633 Squadron and Where Eagles Dare, to name but a few.   *(Andrew Long)*

The author pictured with Lady Bader and Richard Jones at the launch of Missing in Action: Resting in Peace?, Worcester Guildhall, 1998. Other pilots pictured at Gordon Batt, Ron Rayner DFC, Geoffrey Stevens and Peter Fox (courtesy Worcester Evening News).

The Ramrod roadshow at the IWM Duxford, for the launch there of Missing in Action: Resting in Peace? Larry McHale personally displays the flying kit of the period!

Ramrod signing, IWM Duxford Airfield, 1999, appropriately in the former 19 Squadron hangar!. From left to right: Flight Lieutenants Ken Wilkinson and Tony Pickering, Squadron Leader Laurance Thorogood, Bob Morris, John Milne, Ernie French and Fred Roberts.

At Worcester Guildhall, September 2000: Flight Lieutenant Keith Lawrence DFC, Bob Morris, Flight Lieutenant Richard Jones and Ken Wilkinson, Dilip Sarkar, Ernie French, Bill Kirk and Fred Roberts. It is through hosting events at such mainstream venues that the author's vision of bringing the living history of the Battle of Britain to as wide an audience as possible.

B o o k launches also provide an opportunity for 'living h i s t o r y' enthusiasts to add a period flavour. Here, at Worcester Guildhall in May 2002, we have Ray Loveslife-Brown and the author's 10 year old son, James,

as American Airborne, Andy Burley in American Ranger dress uniform, Larry McHale as one of the Few, and Dave Walker as a Ranger on 'D-Day'.

Having achieved the statue of Sir Douglas Bader at Goodwood airfield in 2001, sculptor Kenneth Potts is now working on a statue of the late, great, AVM Johnnie Johnson, to be located at the prestigious RAF Museum, Hendon. At the launch of Johnnie Johnson: Spitfire Top Gun, Part One, the public were actually able to watch the sculptor at work.

Over the years, it has not been all book signings! A massive amount of charity and other work goes on behind the scenes every year, including presentations to schools (which Dilip has been providing at his own expense since 1986). Here Battle of Britain pilot Richard Jones answers questions from a pupil at Dilip's old school, Sibford Ferris, November 2000.

Children from Kempsey Primary School in Worcestershire examine artefacts from the Battle of Britain, November 2001, and at which presentation they were able to ask questions of Battle of Britain pilot Ken Wilkinson and aero-mechanic Bob Morris. Again, these are terrific opportunities for youngsters to actually meet veterans.

Children at a Herefordshire Primary School pose with the DFC of Pilot Officer Jack Hamar, in 1990. A dozen years later, the chances are that they, in adulthood, will still remember that day, proving that the message of the debt we owe can be put across, even so many years after the events in question. We WILL remember them!

The Johnnie Johnson Statue Appeal
*Life-and-a-quarter bronze for the
RAF Museum, Hendon!*

Johnnie Johnson officially became the RAF's top scoring fighter pilot of WW2 with 38 ½ aerial victories. Following Johnnie's death in 2001, Dilip Sarkar felt strongly that a statue should be erected to permanently commemorate this great British hero. Of such projects Dilip already had some experience, his close friend, the sculptor Kenneth Potts ARBS having already created Goodwood Airfield's statue of Sir Douglas Bader, which was unveiled by Lady Bader on August 9th, 2001.

Having achieved the Johnson family's approval and support, Dilip contacted Dr Michael Fopp, Director of the RAF Museum, suggesting that Hendon would make a perfect site for this proposed tribute. Following a meeting with the Director and his staff, approval was granted, the intention being to locate the statue in what will become, under the Museum's significant expansion programme, a large open space outside the front entrance.

The Director's approval, however, was on the basis that the project would have to be funded by an Appeal, organised and overseen by Dilip Sarkar. The cost of the proposed life-and-a-quarter bronze, which Kenneth Potts will create, is estimated at some £60,000. This figure, therefore, is the Appeal target.

All donations, no matter how large or small, are much appreciated, and can be sent to the following address:-

Johnnie Johnson Statue Appeal
16 Kingfisher Close
St Peter's
Worcester WR5 3RY
ENGLAND

Please make cheques etc payable to 'Johnnie Johnson Statue Appeal'. For further information, please contact 01905 767735 (tel & fax), or dil@ramrodbooks.u-net.com

Did YOU Serve with Johnnie Johnson? Would YOU like to contribute to Part Two?

Looking ahead, we need to trace as many veterans as possible who flew or served with Johnnie during his long and distinguished RAF career. Firstly such personalities would be on our VIP invitation list to the statue unveiling. Secondly, Dilip would be most interested to hear any recollections and/or see any relevant photographs that they may have, particularly regarding the period September 1943 – May 1945, which will be covered in *Johnnie Johnson: Spitfire Top Gun, Part Two*.

Ramrod Publications Mailing List

If you have enjoyed this and other books by Dilip Sarkar, you can become a privileged customer through inclusion on our mailing list. This ensures automatic notification of new releases, in advance of both publication and availability to the general public. This provides the best opportunity of purchasing special limited edition copies, which always sell out very quickly and usually through our mailing list.

Please send your postal and/or email addresses to:-

Anita Sarkar
Ramrod Publications
16 Kingfisher Close
St Peter's
Worcester WR5 3RY

Home Front 1940

When we remember wartime days, and think of those at home,
They pulled together in many ways when Britain stood alone.
As Europe's war clouds gathered, we prepared to meet our foe,
Fearful of an outcome, that only God would know.

Through years of cold discomfort and families in discord,
Tragedy and destruction could never be ignored.
The nation rose as one with courage and with pride,
Steadfast determination, to beat the oppressor's tide.

A sense of being together and holding all at bay,
A life of desperate stuggle to live from day-to-day.
To see our homes and loved ones, desecrated, gone,
We knew that we'd not falter, but fight till all was won.

Our famous bulldog spirit, our backs against the wall,
This Home Front that encompassed us would herald evil's fall.
We held our heads erect and proud and never shied away,
Of sacrafice and humour, we had no other way.

Larry McHale, Smallford, February 2002